"I've spoken at hundreds of events fo riage, and I can honestly not think of a more needed book. Is it possible (please!) that we can finally have an honest conversation in the church about the visual nature of men without guys being called creeps and women being called frigid? My deepest prayer is that couples will read this book and be able to talk without judgment about this reality for men in our modern society and for their marriages. For many couples, this will be the most important book they read this year—and maybe in their entire relationship."

—KATHI LIPP, author of *The Husband Project, Happy Habits for Every Couple,* and the Hot Mama series

"Women, be brave. This is all the stuff your man has been trying to tell you about how he's wired, but didn't know how to say. This is the stuff every mom of a boy needs to know. Whether you have an issue you need to address, are curious about how to support a man or guide a son, or simply need reassurance that the male wiring was intended to be a good thing, this resource will help. This eye-opening book is *the* go-to resource for a whole new generation of women who care about men."

—SHANNON ETHRIDGE, MA, relationship coach, speaker, and author of many books including the best-selling Every Woman's Battle series, *The Sexually Confident Wife,* and *The Passion Principles*

"The visual nature of men is an unchangeable reality of life, love, and marriage. And it is an issue few women understand. That lack of knowledge creates a lot of relational problems and barriers to experiencing intimacy. Finally, here is a book that will empower women with the truth about how God made men and how to relate to them with understanding. I love this book and am so thankful to Craig and Shaunti for writing it."

—JIMMY AND KAREN EVANS, co-hosts of the syndicated
television program *MarriageToday with Jimmy and Karen*

"Finally a book to help women understand what even the most honorable man or boy faces today! Many wives personalize a man's visual nature as evidence that her good-willed husband does not love her. Of course, all he can say is 'Well, I do love you' as he battles to avoid the swimming areas and the *Sports Illustrated* swimsuit edition, or to stay accountable with his Internet viewing. And when men have given in to those temptations, and don't understand the pain they inflict on their wives, their wives don't know how to handle it. In *Through a Man's Eyes*, every wife, mom, counselor, and pastor has the resource we've been waiting for."

—EMERSON EGGERICHS, best-selling author of *Love and Respect*

"This is a home-run title on such a desperately needed topic! *Through a Man's Eyes* opened my eyes to so many things that men struggle with and served as the springboard for some very helpful and healthy conversations with my husband. I appreciate the courage Shaunti and Craig had to address this subject and the grace with which they did so. Highly recommended for any woman who wants to understand her husband, son, boyfriend, or other men in her life better."

—CRYSTAL PAINE, founder of MoneySavingMom.com
and *New York Times* best-selling author

"Oh, how I wish I'd had this resource thirty-two years ago when I was a new wife. Even though I've been married for many years, I learned so much on the pages of this book. If you have a man in your life, you need this resource! Thank you, Shaunti and Craig, for giving women the gift of understanding."

—JILL SAVAGE, CEO of Hearts at Home and author
of *No More Perfect Moms*

"Reading this book made me think Craig and Shaunti had somehow installed a hidden camera in my brain! Their insights into the male thought process are incredibly accurate. This book will help women develop a deeper understanding of men, and consequently will create deeper levels of intimacy in their relationships."

—DAVE WILLIS, founder of StrongerMarriages.org and author
of *iVow: Secrets to a Stronger Marriage*

"*Through a Man's Eyes* picks up where *For Women Only* left off, in giving me (Barb) insight into understanding the visual nature of men. For years we've told couples around the world to make sure they buy a copy of the book. This new book is excellent! So compelling we couldn't put it down. Thank you, Shaunti and Craig, for writing more on these crucial differences between men and women. It gives couples everywhere the capacity to talk about them."

—DR. GARY AND BARB ROSBERG, America's Family Coaches

"Any woman (or man!) who reads this book will have a much better understanding of the visual nature of men and boys. As I read this book, words like *refreshing, challenging, insightful, grace, practical,* and *helpful* kept popping into my head. Shaunti and Craig are two of my favorite authors, researchers, and friends, and I respect and admire both of them. Putting these two people together to write this book makes it not only a stroke of genius but a resource that will bring health and understanding to thousands of women who need to comprehend how men think and react to visual stimulation. The answers to the questions about the effect of pornography on men and boys could save many a relationship."

—JIM BURNS, PhD, president of HomeWord and author
of *Teaching Your Kids Healthy Sexuality* and *The Purity Code* (for teens and preteens)

"Men have long needed their hidden sexual wiring exposed along with the challenges it brings. And women have long needed this enlightenment and the compassion for their men that surely comes with it. Clearly, a must-read!"

—DR. ROBERT LEWIS, founder of Men's Fraternity
and producer of *Marriage Oneness*

"This is a book that all husbands should want their wives to read. *Through a Man's Eyes* takes women on a journey into the minds of men and shows them how even nice guys struggle with the onslaught of visual temptation they face every day. Thankfully, it also shows women how to be compassionate, wise, and encouraging in dealing with this aspect of their husbands' lives."

—MARK AND SUSAN MERRILL, founders of Family First,
All Pro Dad, and iMOM

"This is a much-needed book! Every wife, girlfriend, or mom needs to read it and then be encouraged because she has finally cracked the secret code and understands something that is a daily part of life for every male on the planet. Only with true understanding can true intimacy thrive—and this will get you there."

—DRS. LES AND LESLIE PARROTT, authors of *Saving Your Marriage Before It Starts*

shaunti feldhahn & craig gross

through a man's eyes

Helping Women Understand the Visual Nature of Men

MULTNOMAH
BOOKS

THROUGH A MAN'S EYES
PUBLISHED BY MULTNOMAH BOOKS
12265 Oracle Boulevard, Suite 200
Colorado Springs, Colorado 80921

Details in some anecdotes and stories have been changed to protect the identities of the persons involved.

Trade Paperback ISBN 978-1-60142-511-9
eBook ISBN 978-1-60142-512-6

Cover design by Lucy Iloenyosi, Neatworks Inc.

Published in association with the literary agency of Fedd and Company Inc., P.O. Box 341973, Austin, TX 78734.

Published in the United States by WaterBrook Multnomah, an imprint of the Crown Publishing Group, a division of Penguin Random House LLC, New York.

MULTNOMAH and its mountain colophon are registered trademarks of Penguin Random House LLC.

Library of Congress Cataloging-in-Publication Data
Feldhahn, Shaunti.
    Through a man's eyes : helping women understand the visual nature of men / Shaunti Feldhahn and Craig Gross. — First Edition.
        pages cm
    Includes bibliographical references.
    ISBN 978-1-60142-511-9 — ISBN 978-1-60142-512-6 (electronic) 1. Sex—Religious aspects—Christianity. 2. Sex. 3. Men—Sexual behavior. 4. Sexual attraction. 5. Sexual excitement. I. Title.
    BT708.F455 2015
    248.8'43—dc23

                                                    2015008752

Printed in the United States of America
2016

10 9 8 7 6 5 4 3 2

SPECIAL SALES
Most WaterBrook Multnomah books are available at special quantity discounts when purchased in bulk by corporations, organizations, and special-interest groups. Custom imprinting or excerpting can also be done to fit special needs. For information, please e-mail SpecialMarkets@WaterBrook Multnomah.com or call 1-800-603-7051.

From Shaunti:
*To the men and boys who work to take every
thought captive in a challenging culture. On behalf
of wives and moms everywhere, we honor you.*

● ● ● ● ●

From Craig:
*To all wives and mothers. Thank you for taking
the time to understand the inner lives of the males
in your life. We are very grateful for you.*

Contents

1

What Men See

Just for a moment, we want you to step with us into a pair of shoes that, in real life, you will never wear: those of a man in your life. Maybe those shoes belong to your husband or boyfriend. Maybe your son. Maybe your brother or father or close friend.

We want to take you on a tour of what life looks like to men, from the inside.

Why would you want or need this tour?

Because you're not a guy. And as a result, you're missing a huge part of the life experienced by your husband, boyfriend, or son—or any other man in your life (your boss, your pastor, your neighbor). He faces some major challenges. They are in his face. Every. Single. Day. These challenges often come with consequences for him, for you, and for your relationship—yet you might be completely un-aware that they even exist.

Even for the most noble, honorable men, they exist.

Yet once your eyes are opened to these challenges, the potential consequences, and how to handle them, everything changes. You will understand how men see life in certain ways—and *why*. You will understand the impact—both the negative and the positive—that it could have on their relationships with you and others. And you will know what you can do to provide support, prevent problems, and address any issues that have arisen.

But that comes later. For now, set it all aside, and come with us on that tour of what life looks like for men.

Literally *looks* like. We are going to experience a summer day in the life of a fairly typical guy whom we will call Jack. Jack is thirty years old, and he is a good guy who takes his faith seriously. He has been married for two years, doesn't have kids yet, and works in commercial real estate in a midsized city. He went to bed late the night before and has a full day ahead . . .

6:30 a.m.—BEEP! BEEP! BEEP!

After silencing his alarm, Jack reluctantly opens his bleary eyes and lies in bed for a minute, trying to wake up. He hears the shower running in the master bathroom a few feet away and the watery sounds of his wife humming happily. An image of what she looks like right now, standing there in the spray, jumps to his mind, and he feels his body respond. He smiles as he remembers what she looked like in this bedroom late last night, and he savors a few mental images. Yes, they went to sleep a bit later than anticipated . . . but it was worth it!

The sound of the shower shutting off snaps him out of his reverie. Jack swings out of bed and heads toward the bathroom. As he pushes open the door, he sees his wife hastily wrapping a towel around herself—*What a shame*—and smiles at her as he says good morning. He gives her a sweet kiss on top of her wet head. She always looks embarrassed to be seen with no clothes on ("My butt is too big, and my boobs are too small," she always says), but he loves stealing glances at her when he can. He savors every image of her he has, from their wedding night onward.

His brain starts to imagine what she looks like under that towel, but he shuts down that train of thought. No sense making himself crazy; she's running to work and so is he.

Shaking the thought out of his head, he steps into the shower and resolutely forces himself to think about the tasks of the busy day ahead.

8:30 a.m.—Downtown

"Morning." Jack and his colleagues greet each other as they enter the office building. As the elevator doors open onto the third floor, he notes which colleagues are already there and which cubes are empty.

He'll be leaving shortly for the big review meeting at the De-Marco Hotel site and, given the tension with the client, he needs some paperwork from each of his colleagues. But he doesn't see . . .

Cole, where is Cole? I need his numbers before I leave. He said he'd have them to me by now!

For the next hour, he finds it hard to concentrate as his eyes continually flick between the clock and the elevator bank. Then an elevator door opens and his colleague Abbie comes striding down the corridor.

In a nanosecond, it is as if a spotlight is shining on her well-endowed figure and her crisp white blouse. As usual, she seems to have missed doing up those top two buttons. A giant invisible magnet instantly draws Jack's eyes to the top of her lacy bra and the perfect form inside.

And as usual, in that nanosecond he has two powerful forces wrestling within him. He feels a tightening in his gut and a temptation to consume that pleasurable image for as long as he can before Abbie sees him. But he also wants to honor his wife (and God) in his thought life and to respect Abbie as a person and colleague.

Jack wrenches his head away. Knowing Abbie is about to walk directly past his cubicle, he turns his chair slightly so his back faces the door. That way she is less likely to stop for some polite morning chitchat. For a few moments, he stares blankly at the DeMarco Hotel paperwork on his desk, extremely aware of the fact that Abbie is walking past him *right now*. He fights a desire to turn around and take a look at her back view, which is usually interesting too. He breathes a sigh of relief when the sound of her heels fades from earshot.

Now the only problem is that he has to fight several attempts made by *other* images of Abbie—other outfits, other glimpses—to intrude on the screen of his mind. Each time another unbidden image appears, he resolutely refocuses on the DeMarco numbers.

He's having trouble concentrating on them. What else can he think about to distract himself? What's his next task again?

Oh right! Cole's numbers! He looks back to the elevator just as Cole rushes in. Jack quickly intercepts his colleague to get his report, then heads out the door.

9:47 a.m.—Somewhere on the highway

Jack hates this stretch of road. In order to get to the new resort hotel site, he has to drive fifty miles outside the city. And at least ten billboards along the way advertise so-called gentlemen's clubs. He has never been to one, but multiple television shows and movies have shown girls dancing around stripper poles, which sends his memory back to those images whenever a new billboard appears.

On each billboard, the smoldering eyes of the fifteen-foot-high seductive woman try to draw his gaze—eyes that say *I want you.* Since Jack can't look the other direction for too long without crashing the car, he does what his dad once taught him to do. He keeps his eyes resolutely on the road and prays for the young women who are trapped in those professions.

And a few miles on, he does that again.

And again.

And again.

10:30 a.m.—The new resort hotel site, outside the city

As Jack steps out of his car and begins walking down the path between the new hotel and the one next door, he hears some boisterous young voices. About ten yards ahead of him, he sees five or six teenage girls come out of the hotel next door and head toward the pool. All are wearing bikinis and have clearly been in and out of the pool a few times already.

Jack again feels that desire to look. Because he's behind the girls, he could look with impunity and feel the pleasure of consuming all those exhilarating images.

But thankfully, he has ammunition. He looks away from the girls and calls to mind instead that other intoxicating image. That one of his wife last night. He savors it like a delicious drink for a moment, allowing his mind to view it in slow motion. By the time the path reaches the doors of the hotel, the girls are no longer in sight—he lost track of where they went—and he is grinning to himself and feeling a great rush of affection for his wife.

11:15 a.m.—Halfway through the meeting

Jack is trying to sort through the contradictory numbers and differing stories shared by his on-site manager and the hotel manager. Were the cost overruns actually authorized by the client, or weren't they?

His client pauses the meeting for a second to send a quick text message to someone. He tells Jack, "I've just asked Dionne, our financial officer, to come in and share her paper trail so you see that we simply never approved these additional expenditures."

A moment later, the door opens, and Jack does a double take, then relaxes.

Dionne is a beautiful woman with flowing dark hair, chocolate-brown eyes, and an eye-catching white suit. And even in that split second Jack can tell that she probably has a great figure. But Dionne is polished and professional without being provocative. Her suit is pretty, but it isn't tight. Her top doesn't show a thing. And when she sits down next to Jack to work through a series of spreadsheets, her skirt is long enough that it doesn't ride up.

Jack breathes a sigh of relief and then focuses on the complex numbers as she takes him through the client's version of the paper trail.

Thirty minutes later he isn't fully convinced, but it is clear Dionne has done her homework and she has made a good case. He stands up, shakes her hand, and tells her so.

"I can't promise we will come down on your side, but we're

going to take a much harder look at some of these numbers," he says as he takes his leave.

1:00 p.m.—Back at the downtown office

The next few hours are tough. Back at the office, he has trouble concentrating on what Abbie is saying as she and Cole walk him through the other side of the DeMarco numbers. And later, when images of Abbie's form pop up in his mind, he resolutely tears them down by thinking about his wife, the DeMarco numbers, or getting the car transmission serviced. And then during his break, he has to deal with the sidebar pop-ups on various social media sites during the few moments he spends online.

Next there's the after-work trip through the auto shop where the magazines in the waiting room include old copies of *Maxim*. Jack stands up and walks around for a while . . . until he realizes that the pictures on the walls include pinups. And during the drive home, the news radio station airs a commercial for "the little pill . . . when the time is right"—and images of when the time *was* right begin to play in his brain.

By the time Jack pulls into the driveway, it is nearly 8:00 p.m., and he's hungry for more than just food. After dinner, as he helps clean up the kitchen, he comes up behind his wife and gives her a big hug and his hands begin to wander. She playfully slaps his hand and chuckles, "You only have one thing on your mind, don't you? Hey, I was going to tell you, Scott and Josie are interested in looking at the bikes this weekend if you really do want to sell them . . ."

Jack smiles ruefully to himself and drags his mind back to what his wife is saying, and away from where it wants to go.

But maybe tomorrow night . . .

A Normal Guy in an Abnormal Situation

Jack is not a sex addict, not a pervert, and he doesn't have any unusual problems with his thought life. He is a normal man in an abnormal situation. He is living with a visually wired and stimulated brain in a culture filled with very public images that were only meant to be seen in private.

The reason we wanted to give you this peek (so to speak) into a day in Jack's life is that because men and women are wired so differently, women often don't realize how the opposite sex sees the world.

> Men are living with visually wired and stimulated brains in a culture filled with very public images that were only meant to be seen in private.

Most women simply aren't aware of what *man's visual nature* even means, or how much it impacts literally every area of most men's lives and relationships. And ironically, because men often aren't aware that women aren't aware of this part of their lives, they may not ever talk about it, or know how to explain it if they do.

It is vital to fill in this blind spot so that we can grasp the challenges men face every day in this culture, why they see the world this way, and the amount of work it takes to keep their thought lives pure.

And once we see what they see, we can begin to understand what to do about it: how to support the man or boy we love, how to prevent problems from starting, and what to do if someone we care about has fallen into some of the common traps of our modern culture.

Unfortunately, I (Shaunti) have seen that most of us have absolutely no idea just how crucial this understanding is. Both in my work as a social researcher and speaker, and in Craig's work as the founder of XXXchurch.com, we have noticed this irony: men are visual . . . and women are blind to it. All too often, we simply don't see—or we completely misunderstand—a man's visual nature. Just when we need the most thorough possible understanding of men, we are the most clueless.

This disconnect would be merely amusing if the consequences weren't so serious. Consequences like a ten-year-old boy (an age where intervention is the easiest) being drawn to search for "boobs" on Google Images . . . but because his mom doesn't know how to handle it, she does nothing. Consequences like that same ten-year-old boy, six years later, wanting to try certain things with his girlfriend that he never would have thought of on his own—and his girlfriend, in her confusion, assuming it must be normal and going along with it.

Consequences like a twenty-three-year-old woman breaking up with the man she thought she would marry, because he confessed he had looked at *Maxim* magazine a few times. Or the forty-year-old husband with a deep need for more intimacy whose wife is offended and pulls away when he tries clumsily to explain just how much he wants more thoughts of *her* in his mind, rather than all the other images he sees around him.

Consequences like the woman who, after discovering that her husband struggles with porn, spirals into depression or considers divorce because she blames herself or thinks he doesn't love her. Or even consequences like the business leader, pastor, or schoolteacher who desperately wants his female staff members or audience to understand

> Learning how to be an active support and partner is one of the greatest gifts you can give the man or boy in your life today.

issues with certain attire . . . but gives up because he has no idea how to explain it in a way that doesn't make him sound like a creep.

In today's culture, *a man's visual nature impacts every area of his life*. Home, work, school, church, sports, leisure activities, marriage, dating, parenting, prayer, friendships—nothing is exempt. And because it impacts every area of his life, it impacts our life as well.

Learning how to be an active support and partner is one of the greatest gifts you can give the man or boy in your life today. It can be life-changing in a way we never would have imagined. And that is why we wanted to write this book.

A Bit About Us

Both of us writing this book come at life and this subject from a Christian perspective. All the information here is based on the best and most rigorous scientific, psychological, and practical resources available—including some of our own research that is used widely in the general market—but our approach in this book has a clear faith-based thread. It will include our best effort to discern the callings and responsibilities of those who not only want to honor each other but also want to honor God.

So here's a bit about us.

I (Shaunti) am a wife, mom of two (ages twelve and fifteen), and social researcher who is probably best known for a book called *For Women Only: What You Need to Know About the Inner Lives of Men* and other research-based books about men, women, teens, the workplace, and relationships. Today, in addition to researching and writing, I speak at women's conferences, churches, marriage semi-nars, corporate conventions, and other events. I love seeing the life change that comes when people get something simple but important that they just didn't know before.

And I (Craig) am a husband, a father of two children (ages ten and twelve), and the founder of a ministry called XXXchurch that helps men and women all over the world who struggle with pornography and sexual sin. I have a lot of experience in helping people who are caught up in that world, and I spend a good amount of my time speaking at churches, conferences, and colleges talking about pornography, sex addictions, and temptations. Later in this book I'll be addressing a series of questions that we get asked frequently at XXX church.com—questions from women just like you. I tend to be pretty blunt and don't sugarcoat the truth, but I don't mean to offend, upset, or shock you by that. I'm really glad you're reading this book, and I'm delighted to take part in helping you understand where the man in your life is coming from.

How We Got Here—and Why We Are Writing This Book

When I (Shaunti) first stumbled into this field of social research, I was realizing just how much I as a woman didn't understand about men. What it means when we say "Men are visual" was at the top of the list.

My journey started years ago when I was writing a novel and didn't know how to articulate the thoughts of my main male character in a scene similar to the one involving Jack and Abbie. I asked some men I trusted what they would be thinking in such a situation, purely so I could make sure I accurately described the thoughts of a man . . . and I found myself shocked by their answers. These godly men described thoughts, feelings, and—most important—images that were completely foreign to me. And a bit alarming! Yet I trusted this group of men, which included my husband.

Once I set out to understand this reality much more thoroughly, it snowballed. I ended up with a comprehensive look not only into the visual nature of men but also into all the vital things that we women tend not to get about men—things men wish we knew and, in many cases, think we already *do* know! And the research has continued. I've interviewed and commissioned nationally representative surveys of more than six thousand men over twelve years for various books.

This male visual wiring was just one of the eight truths I explored in *For Women Only*. But it is by far the topic that leads to the most e-mails, blog posts, online comments, and questions during my speaking events or radio interviews. The same has been true for Craig as he speaks at churches and universities and is regularly interviewed as an expert on news outlets like CNN.

The reactions from women readers and listeners range from deep thankfulness at finally understanding their man's wiring to worrisome misunderstandings. They run the gamut from stunned curiosity (like mine) or relief that their man is normal, all the way to anger that "you are telling men it's okay to look" (which we are *not,* by the way!) or overwrought tears with the question "How can I ever trust him again now that I know he's tempted to look at other women?"

And along with those reactions is a clear need, not just to more specifically understand this aspect of a husband, boyfriend, or son, but for more specific guidance on how to be a better wife, girlfriend, or mom in this area and how to head off certain challenges and address others once they have arisen.

That is what we will be giving you in the pages ahead. And that is why this is a book that is written for women. It is fine for men to take a look, to see what we are telling their wives or girlfriends, but the goal of this book is to educate, equip, and where necessary, exhort women to understanding and action.

We'll be taking you on a very specific journey . . . not simply to awareness and action, but also to encouragement and hope. God specifically created men to be visual. Despite the challenges this poses for men in this fallen world and our sexualized culture, the gift of this wiring is ultimately intended to be a good thing, not a bad one.

It is also something that is as diverse and individual as every man, every boy, and every marriage. We will be largely focusing on those things that affect the majority of men and/or cause the most significant issues, but there will be many exceptions. And it is vital to use this information as a *starting point* for understanding the men and boys in your life—including the unique way each of them is wired as an individual.[1] It is also vital to realize that because this is a starting point, there are certain things we simply won't be able to cover in detail. Some are touched on in the Frequently Asked Questions (FAQ) section at the end of the book; we will provide resources for others at our website, MenAreVisual.com.

We know that this subject can be awkward to talk about and even read about. We will do our best to address it matter-of-factly but with sensitivity and respect for men and for you.

Who Should Read This Book

If any of the following statements describe you, we think the knowledge in this book is important and has the potential to be life changing for how you relate to and support your husband, boyfriend, or son in a difficult culture:

- You want to have your eyes opened to these sometimes-awkward truths.
- You are curious and want to know the real deal about men before you start dating.
- You are willing and able to look at the positives of how God created men.
- You have learned that the man or boy in your life has a problem and you want to understand why and how this happened, and what to do now.
- You can handle any challenging things you learn.

That last statement brings us to an important point. Before we get started, we want to ask you to do one thing: make sure you are ready or able to read this book. If you are feeling ultra-vulnerable, very scared, or are already resentful at the idea of learning what it means that men are visual . . . please don't read this book right now. Come back to it another time.

Both of us have seen that when we explain these truths, some listeners or readers get extremely angry or are devastated because they think we are saying things that, in fact, we would *never* say. Some believe that we are making excuses for men, that we are saying "boys will be boys"; others claim we are blaming women, putting the onus on women to change, or even implying that men are not responsible for their actions. Several have told us, "I'm never going to be able to trust my husband again, now that I know how visual he is," and more than a few devastated husbands have told us that their wives stopped being intimate with them altogether once they learned the truth about how men are wired.

All of those reactions indicate a misunderstanding of our message and our hearts in this book. But we do understand that sometimes a reader might be misreading our words because she is simply in a particularly vulnerable place. If so, it would be wiser for her to wait and learn this information once she can do so without causing herself and her relationships pain.

So please pray before you start reading. Examine your heart to see if you are open to seeing the wonderful ways God created men, even those things that might be hard to hear. And pray about how to support the men—husband, brother, son, father, coworker, pastor—in your life.

If, at any point, you start to freak out a bit as you read, stop and pray before you continue. Remind yourself that your husband, boyfriend, or son is the same person he was five minutes ago, but now you know something he's been dealing with all along—something he didn't know how to explain, didn't want to explain, or was afraid to explain. We think true love means knowing and supporting each other, and our prayer is that this book will help you do that in a wonderful way that will bring you closer.

> True love means knowing and supporting each other, and our prayer is that this book will help you do that in a wonderful way that will bring you closer.

● ● ● ● ●

So if you are ready, let's jump in. Let's start by looking at why men are so visual and the amazing way God has created their brains to be so different from ours.

2

Why Men
Are So Visual

The man in your life is wired very differently than you.

Okay, you probably figured that out already.

But the type of *wiring* we're talking about is different from the usual use of that term. We don't mean just he thinks differently than you or has a different set of needs and insecurities, although both are true and we'll tackle those shortly. Rather, we literally mean that at the most basic level, the structure of the male brain is physically different from that of the female brain. In many ways, it also has a completely different chemical-hormonal mix. And that physical and chemical composition, and process, which we refer to as brain wiring, leads to different tendencies in how men think and feel. Men tend to perceive the world in a certain way, and women tend to perceive the world in a certain way; those two methods of perception overlap in some areas and are wildly different in others. While external and internal factors do contribute to these differences—like the genes you inherited from your parents or all the experiences you've had in your life up to this point—those factors don't explain everything.

The brain is a strange, mysterious, ever-shifting place that even neuroscientists don't understand completely. Craig knows someone who recently got his doctorate in neuroscience who has said many times, "You have no idea how much we still don't know about the brain." And this is a man who has done nothing but study brains for years!

But brain scientists do know some things from research breakthroughs in recent years. And the structural, hormonal, and processing differences between men and women are glaring.

A leading researcher recently summarized the findings of a landmark study of gender differences on the brain[2] by saying that the old, lingering notion that, "sex does not matter to brain function . . . has been crushed under the weight of evidence proving that it can and regularly does and at every level of investigation."[3]

I (Shaunti) can remember watching a news report a few years ago where a neuroscientist said that the brains of men and women were so different from each other that studying their brains was almost like looking at two different species! Now, if we really are that distinct, you'd think we would be more aware of it. But when it comes to the way we process visual information, we really aren't. Also, we women often don't know how men think or feel, and men don't know that we don't know. And vice versa. And this leads to all sorts of confusion, miscommunication, and frustration precisely because each of us thinks things are perfectly clear and don't realize our mate is seeing things completely differently.

The differences between men and women often mean that instead of coming together, teaming up, and supporting one another in a difficult culture, we end up with misunderstandings, missed opportunities, heartache, hurt feelings, and lonely struggles that never had to happen. Yet once we are aware of certain truths about each other, we have fantastic opportunities for closeness, bonding, mutual support and understanding, and much greater intimacy.

But, all too often, we just don't know some key things. And what we don't know about a man's visual nature is near the top of the list!

To Start Us Off

Although it is important to understand all the visual aspects of men, we have to start with their brain wiring and how different it is from ours. Everything else rests on that foundation, since the brain wiring explains *why* men see the world the way they do.

Keep in mind that I (Shaunti) am simplifying something extremely complicated—something that even brain scientists don't completely understand—and I'm also making some generalizations. Some men are less visually wired, and some women are more so. We are all individuals. The key is to understand the individual guys in *your* life, wherever they are on the visual spectrum. At a very rough estimate, based on my research, this little primer probably describes the brain wiring of at least 90 percent of men and boys to one degree or another.[4]

Men Are All Eyes in Many Ways

According to the latest brain science, the structure and the chemical makeup of the male brain make it impossible for a guy to *not* be visually oriented. Much of how he processes life—even what he thinks and feels—is tied to what he sees.

By contrast, the brains of women have a very different focus: our brains are wired for emotional and verbal processing in a way that is very different from men.

To help you understand what I mean, let me ask some questions: Do you want to talk about the things you experience day to day? Do you have feelings about those things? For example, imagine that your best friend at work suddenly undermined you in front of your colleagues. Or imagine that you saw your normally stoic son tenderly hugging your daughter today after she hurt herself. Would you have emotions spilling over about those day-to-day things? Would you want to recount what happened or share what you felt with someone?

If you're like most women, you answered yes to those questions. You just *are* emotionally and verbally oriented. It is part of you. You could no sooner turn off that part of you than you could turn off your sense of smell.

Well, in the same way, a man can't imagine *not* being visual. It is a huge part of his life. It is even a huge part of his brain: scientists have found that much more of the male brain is set aside for visual processing than in the female brain.[5]

And that visual orientation is especially attuned to sexual images. (A huge shocker, I know.) In fact, his visual nature—combined with testosterone and other brain chemicals that affect memory, sexual bonding, and emotions—makes a guy far more likely to perceive certain sights as sexual in nature in the first place.[6]

This same wiring also means that his initial reaction to those images is far more likely to be instantaneous arousal: a gut-level, pleasurable, *automatic* reaction. In fact most women have never experienced the same sort of involuntary, gut-level, instinctive physical reaction of pleasure to visual and sexual images that many men experience daily. And since most of us have never experienced it, we have no idea that men do.

That seemingly small gap in our understanding, it turns out, has huge consequences—and is one of the main gaps we are trying to bridge with this book.

The Unseen Process

So here's what happens in the actual brain of the average man or boy when he sees an image that he perceives as sexual.

It all starts in an area deep in the back of the brain and involves the brain's mechanism for automatically processing all sorts of pleasurable signals. When you eat a great dessert, for example, you don't think about enjoying its taste; it just happens. In response to that trigger (eating that dessert), several areas of the brain light up, then send signals that cause you (a millisecond later) to recognize the flavor as sweet.

Well, something similar happens when, for example, a man sees a woman who is dressed so as to show off her good figure. A center in the brain called the nucleus accumbens lights up, and a whole chain of events happens within a few seconds.[7]

In order to understand this, let's go back to the food example and examine how everyone (male or female) reacts to a different type of stimulus. The nucleus accumbens is also the part of the brain that lights up when you haven't eaten all day and are famished, then walk into a dinner party and spot a tantalizing buffet. The moment you see the wide array of yummy-looking dishes, you have an instantaneous, physical reaction. You're hungry, you may salivate, and boy, you want to consume that food!

In that first millisecond, you aren't politely thinking, *Oh, how very pleasing that food looks.* Nope, it is an instinctive *I want that,* with (at first) zero thought involved. And just as important: in that first millisecond, you can't *not* have that automatic reaction. It just happens. That is your nucleus accumbens lighting up.

What comes next, though, is just as important. Immediately after that happens in the back of your brain, your cortical (thinking) centers kick in at the front of your brain. This is where your thought process, will, and decision making occur. So one second after your instant hungry reaction, you notice that the buffet is untouched. *Man, dinner hasn't started yet.*

You can now rapidly think things through and make a decision: Go over and stuff your face with chocolate? Or wait politely, keeping a lid on your hunger, until your host says it's time to eat?

In other words: the first draw is automatic and purely biological, *then* you have a choice of what to do about it.

You can probably guess how this relates to the visual male brain.

What He Experiences

When a man walks into a room and sees that hypothetical woman who is dressed in a way that calls attention to her great figure, the man's nucleus accumbens lights up, and he has an involuntary, biological, gut-level reaction of pleasure from seeing that image and a desire to consume that image. Not a desire for that *person* exactly, but the *image.* Just as you would instinctively be drawn to consume the food, he is instinctively drawn to savor that image because it would feel really good to do so.

But a moment later the thinking centers in his brain kick in, and now he has a choice. Does he decide to experience the pleasure of looking at that attractive woman who is showing off all her assets? Or does he look away to honor God—and his wife, if he's married—in his thought life? (Or maybe he and his wife are the only members of the dinner party, and he can look all he wants!)

Although neuroscience shows that the very first reaction is instinctive and biological rather than voluntary,[8] *the next step is a choice.* This is where a man moves from temptation to a healthy, righteous action—or from temptation to sin.

Now consider our friend Jack from the opening chapter. Remember how a giant unseen magnet drew his attention to the unbuttoned top of his colleague Abbie's blouse, what was *inside* the blouse, and the tightening he felt in his gut? That was his nucleus accumbens lighting up: his brain automatically experienced pleasure at the sight. But then his thought process kicked in, and he decided to wrench his head away. He also went one step further and turned his chair, not because he was offended by her attire, but to help himself not look. He was aware of Abbie, but he chose to honor God and his wife in his thought life. He also chose to honor Abbie, both by trying to avoid the temptation to begin with and by working to not think of her in that way.

> Although neuroscience shows that the very first reaction is instinctive and biological rather than voluntary, *the next step is a choice.*

The reason we don't understand a man's draw toward these female images is because our brains process the image of an attractive male very differently.

What Women Experience

In most cases, when a woman sees an attractive man, her nucleus accumbens doesn't light up. There is no automatic, gut-level reaction. Instead, visual attraction usually starts in the cortical centers— meaning it is a thinking-oriented response from the beginning. She *thinks* to herself, *Wow, he's an attractive man.*

In other words, most women have never experienced that initial, involuntary, sensually pleasurable reaction that men feel when they see certain types of images, so we have no idea that it even exists or that it is the way men are legitimately wired. Now, note that I said "most." There are some women who are visual in a similar way, but it's not quite as typical.[9]

We also don't realize how intense a man's reaction is. According to the latest brain science research, the gut-level reaction men have to a sexual image is also quite a bit stronger than the thinking-oriented reaction of women.[10] And the strength of that sight and that reaction can even impact how the brain processes those images over time.[11]

It is also important to note that a man's reaction is different if the image is *attractive* but isn't perceived as *sexual*. Men are able to appreciate beauty just like we are, after all, and that includes noticing that a woman is attractive—without any physical reaction. If a man sees an attractive woman who is *not* calling overt attention to her body, it is often a nonissue. His nucleus accumbens simply doesn't light up. The automatic reaction, and thus temptation, isn't triggered. Without having to work at it, he can mind his own business and go about his day.

God Created Men and Women to Be Different

We need to recognize the most important reason why men are visual. Their brain structure didn't just pop into existence by chance: *God designed them this way.*

Recognizing that one fact can help us adjust to this new knowledge. As we have mentioned, we have experienced a variety of reactions from women as they process this revelation, so we know some of you are a bit freaked out or upset, while others are just shrugging, thinking, *What's the big deal?*

Some of you also may question whether God intentionally created men to be visual in this way. You may argue that this visual wiring exists solely because sin entered the world. That is a legitimate argument; perhaps Adam's brain *wasn't* initially wired to visually appreciate Eve in all her glory. But given that Adam's first words when he saw Eve were essentially "Hubba hubba!" we are inclined to believe God created men in this way, and that this visual wiring was intended to be a wonderful thing—for multiple reasons.

One reason, presumably, is so a man will be biologically attracted to a healthy mate with whom he can "be fruitful and multiply." But it goes beyond that. God likely also provided this visual wiring to help create a wonderful bond between a husband and his wife.

Remember: *The only sexual sight a man was ever supposed to see was of his wife.* Given what you now know, you can grasp the feelings of attachment, delight, and bonding that these sights and memories create in a man toward his wife.

Yes, this culture is challenging for our men. But that attachment, delight, and bonding *with us* is still there. We can still enjoy bonding in this way with our husbands. We can still find ways to teach our sons to try to keep their thought lives pure and save those sights for marriage. We don't have to embrace the cultural belief that guys are just wired to look so it's not a big deal. We don't have to give in to the suspicion that a husband or boyfriend who has always been honorable might be looking at another woman (*Where are his eyes? Did he just look sideways at the girl in the other checkout lane?*). We don't have to give in to the temptation to despair, wondering how we'll ever trust him to be faithful.

> God likely also provided this visual wiring to help create a wonderful bond between a husband and his wife.

We also don't have to give in to the notion that men's visual nature naturally objectifies women (*Guys think we're not people; we're just bodies to be lusted after*). It is not his visual nature that does that; rather, the choice he makes does that. On the contrary, when a man handles this temptation well, he begins to build habits of respect toward women.

Let's address this whole subject as wise women who care about the males in our lives and who want to know—as best we can—how to support them in the world in which we live today.

3

Just Because They Want to Look Doesn't Make Them Jerks

I (Craig) was just a preteen kid when I first discovered the raw, gut-level thrill of seeing the naked feminine form. As these stories often go, I was at a friend's house after school, hanging out with him in his backyard, when he pulled out a *Playboy* magazine that he had found at the park earlier that day. Now, *Playboy* was porn, to be sure, but compared to what is out there now, it was relatively tame.

I can't remember a ton of things from childhood, but I can remember some of these images as if I saw them yesterday. I still remember the instinctive thrill in my heart and my developing loins when I saw those women. Yes, there was an aspect of forbidden fruit to all this—I was, after all, secretly looking at a dirty magazine at my friend's house—but that was a side thrill. Most of what I felt was purely biological.

I didn't turn into a rampaging porn addict, nor did I become a lustful monster who wanted to undress every woman with my eyes.

I was just a kid whose brain was working the way God intended . . . and I stayed a kid whose brain worked the way God intended.

I know it is difficult to grasp (and you might want to take a deep breath here), but this is one thing that your son, husband, and father all have in common: *Most guys like looking at women. And they like looking at or imagining naked women.* They may or may not actually do it, but something deep down inside them sure wants to.

This is true whether the male in question is age nine or ninety, whether he is a godly guy who tries to keep his thought life pure, or the playboy with a standing subscription to the magazine of the same name. This is true whether he is the teenager who tries to refrain from looking at all the bikinis on the beach or the jerk who leers at every woman walking down the street. And of course there is a wide spectrum of men in between. The difference is that the generally honorable guy will at least *try* to reserve those looks and those thoughts for his wife (or future wife), whereas another sort of man has absolutely no problem giving his coarser thoughts free rein.

This also means that today's sexualized culture is actually pretty comfortable for the jerk to live in—and pretty difficult for the guy who wants to be honorable. It also means, unfortunately, that some otherwise good guys have become trapped in habits that are destructive, unhealthy, and painful to you. But just because the *actions* of your husband or son may have become less than honorable, it doesn't mean he is a callous person who doesn't care. It doesn't mean he isn't a good guy in many other ways. A married man who is struggling, for example, almost certainly loves his wife, and he *wants* to honor her in his thought life. He just doesn't always succeed.

Just so you know, this does not in any way excuse wrong choices. And that blanket statement covers everything we'll be sharing in this entire book. No matter what temptation he faces, every man or boy must take the responsibility for his actions. But since this is a book for women, it is essential to learn what being visual means, without flinching from the reality that even the nicest and most respectful men face temptation in today's culture.

Since it can be difficult to grasp how any nice guy could wrestle with this, let's explore a few truths about how a man's visual wiring plays out in his interactions with the world. While we'll reference some facts about boys in this chapter, our primary focus here is on what this looks like for adult men. (We'll come back to what this means for your son in later chapters.) So here are a few truths to grasp.

There's a Difference Between Temptation and Sin

Keep in mind that there is an important difference between temptation and sin—in other words, between temptation and lustful thoughts or actions. The unavoidable temptations we face in our lives *are not sin*. Remember this vital statement from the Bible: "[Jesus] has been tempted in all things as we are, yet without sin."[12]

Jesus was certainly not a jerk. But if He was indeed tempted in every way that we are, that means if Jesus ever happened across a scantily clad pagan temple prostitute, He, as a fully human male, would presumably have had that back-of-the-brain automatic reaction. And He would have been tempted to look. And yet if He did indeed have that temptation, we can be assured that He handled it well, which is the same way that our men are called to handle it.[13]

A Man Likes Looking at His Woman

If you are married, your husband loves to look at you, whether you realize it or not. He finds great pleasure in stealing sideways glimpses when you are wearing something attractive . . . or nothing at all. He stores up those images to think about later.

And let's be explicit: he's not just stealing glimpses of your face. Even if you've been married for thirty years and your bikini days are long past, he is still enjoying the sight of your curves. I (Craig) know you might find that hard to believe, but I can tell you from hundreds of conversations with men that it is very true. Men don't see things the same way you women do. You may think that in the privacy of his heart, he really isn't enjoying looking at you because you don't look like you did when you got married. But for most guys, that simply isn't true, especially if you are making some type of effort to take care of yourself. I've been married a long time, and my wife and I have had two kids together, and I still think she's the hottest woman in the world. She is more of a knockout to me now than she's ever been. Although she has all the usual feminine doubts about whether I really mean it, I do. And for those of you who are married, be assured that your husband does too.

> If you are married, your husband loves to look at you, whether you realize it or not.

His Attraction to Other Images Has Nothing to Do with You

Now, I (Shaunti) know what some of you are thinking: *But what about those other images? The ones that aren't me?* If you are married or dating, you may be irritated or hurt by the thought that your man could be physically attracted to someone other than you. After all, if you're like most women (although not all!), you can notice that the male movie star on the cover of *People* magazine is very *attractive*—

and yet have absolutely no personal, physical *attraction* toward him or his body, much less any desire to absorb every detail of his image. You don't know him or truly want to be with him. There's no sense of being drawn or attracted to him as a person. So why would you be drawn in that way to his picture?

In our female way of thinking, a person would only feel that pull if they cared about and were attracted to someone *as a person*. For us, attraction is certainly visual to some degree, but it is also highly emotional. In fact, in our emotional and physical wiring, true attraction inextricably becomes connected to closeness and intimacy with one person. Thus, once we are deeply attached to one person emotionally, we would have to *allow* ourselves to be truly attracted to someone else—and that feels terribly wrong. As one marriage ministry leader summed it up, "Because you love your husband, you cannot imagine looking at the male anatomy like that—cannot imagine even being tempted. So you assume that if your husband *is* tempted like that, that he is allowing himself to be, which you think means he must not really love you." If this sounds logical to us as women, it's only because we have a deep misunderstanding about men.

A man can have a physical attraction toward an image, but *it is not the same thing that we experience as attraction*. In the vast majority of cases, he is attracted to the image alone, and to the sense of pleasure an image gives him; he is not attracted to the *person*. Here is one man's helpful explanation:

> Yes, most men are prone to notice and can't not notice, but
> we don't go through our days going "I wish that woman was
> mine" or "I'd love to have sex with that woman right now." I
> can be out shopping for light bulbs or something, and see the
> hot woman walk into Target who is dressed in all the wrong

ways, and can be very aware that she's in the store some-where . . . but it doesn't mean I wish I was with her. After all, a guy loves his wife or girlfriend, and that other image is just an *image.* I care nothing about her. And just because there is a part of me that is stimulated by that sight doesn't mean I want it to be. It doesn't mean I want to have sex with her! At least that is the case for most guys who usually work to shut down those thoughts. Now, yes, teenage boys will wrestle with that thought! But that age is also when you start trying to turn off those thoughts, or you'd never accomplish any-thing else in life. So once you're an adult in your twenties or thirties, it's like, yeah, you see that type of woman and you have to be on guard for it, and that is pretty much it.

This Attraction Is Present in Boys at the Earliest Age

It is hard for many of us to believe that the initial visual pleasure—and temptation—is truly involuntary and biological, even for guys who want to do the right thing. It can help to understand that this visual awareness and resulting desire are present even in very young boys who have no concept of sex—and yet have exactly the same type of physical pleasure and draw that we've been talking about here.

I'm sure I'm not the only mom to have seen this type of thing. One woman told me that she took her three-year-old son with her to a fabric store, where she browsed the sewing patterns while he sat on a chair and looked at the pictures in his book. At least she thought he was looking at his book. Unbeknownst to her, he found the sewing-pattern images of the women in their underwear much more fascinating. A few minutes later he yelled across the crowded store, "Mom! Every time I look at these girls my pee-pee stands up!"

This little boy was three years old and had no idea what sex was . . . but he still had a male brain.

Stimulating Images Are Impossible to Avoid

The problem, of course, is that this culture is saturated with images that the brains of our men and our sons cannot avoid and that leave them in a constant state of stimulation. Every mall, parking lot, or television show is a minefield—from the photographs in the Victoria's Secret store windows to the packs of beautiful girls in cheerleading shorts at sports events to the sexy images on beer commercials that flash up on the screen and are gone before a guy can look away.

And because women aren't wired the same way, we don't tend to notice the minefield in the same way. While we may notice the skimpy bikinis on the beach, we don't have any concept of how much the male brain is wired to enjoy looking at that sea of almost-naked bodies—even if the man himself tries not to. While we may comment "Look at what that gal is wearing!" (or may envy her great figure!), we don't realize it's just one more thing that stimulates his brain in a way that he may not want.

When I was doing the research for *For Young Women Only* to help teenage girls understand how guys think—and why their parents keep bugging them about not dressing "that way"—I spoke to one college-age guy who provided a great analogy:

> Girls need to know what they're doing to guys when they
> tempt them, visually. A girl's equivalent might be how she
> responds to touch. How would you feel if guys were able to

come up and touch you, all day long, whenever they wanted to? How much would you be able to concentrate on school? Well, when you are dressing to emphasize your figure, you are doing that same thing to guys. You're stimulating them visually to the same degree you would be stimulated by constant touch.

Let me (Craig) go further. Imagine how frustrating it would be to be constantly stimulated in that way and *not want to be.* Imagine that you go to the mall and every fifteen minutes while you're walking the hallways or sitting at the food court, an attractive guy walks by you and runs his fingers over the skin of your arm as he passes, or reaches over and puts his hand on your knee. Your physiology is designed to be stimulated by that touch, so it may feel good, but this is happening without your consent and you don't want to be stimulated by these total strangers.

That is how many men who want to be honorable describe this culture and what it is like for guys.

Now, at this point you might be confused. *Wait a minute,* you wonder. *You said that guys* want *to look, but can choose not to. But here you're saying they don't want to. So which is it?*

Here's the deal: As a male humanoid, he instinctively and biologically wants to look because it would feel good to do so. But as a caring husband, father, or honorable member of society, he *doesn't want to want to look.* As one man told us via e-mail:

> Imagine how frustrating it would be to be constantly stimulated in that way and *not want to be.* That is how many men who want to be honorable describe this culture.

It is as if part of me wants to do X and part of me wants to do Y. For example, as a father, there are days when the selfish part of me thinks life would be a whole lot easier without kids. The other part of me, of course, can't imagine life without them! Both are real, but I choose to honor the "good dad" part and keep it front and center, and push away and try to transform the part of me that wants to live selfishly.

This [visual] issue is similar. There is part of me that wants to look at that woman, and fantasize and enjoy the thrill of that, but the best in me wants to see her as a beautiful, precious woman created by God to be someone's wife, someone's daughter. The key is which part of me I keep front and center. Every man has to wrestle with that.

Do you see the heart behind his words? In this culture, every man has to wrestle with it, but most truly don't want to have to deal with constantly fighting that battle.

As one man put it, "It is exhausting. It is constantly there, in your face. Sometimes you do a better job than others at tuning it out, or turning your eyes away when you can't tune it out." He shrugged ruefully. "But when it is always *there,* there's only so much you can do. You just have to deal with it."

Another man spoke for many: "I've been trying to explain to my daughters why, in their words, I 'hassle' them about what they wear: because many guys wish we could just turn off this part of our brains, but we can't. When I am out minding my own business and the girl in the short shorts saunters by, my brain is being invaded without my consent. I *hate* the constant need to shoot down those thoughts. I tell my daughters that guys really respect women who don't add to the minefield."

Even the church can be a minefield. When a pastor is doing a series on relationships and wants to help the women in the congregation understand men, I (Shaunti) frequently am interviewed during the Sunday morning sermon time. I've lost track of the number of pastors who have asked me to *please* explain this visual issue to the women in the congregation because it is so difficult for the pastor or the men on the worship team or in the congregation who are trying to teach, listen, pray, sing, or worship God . . . when right in front of them there's a woman wearing a really low-cut top.

At this point, you may wonder why that would be a big deal. *Okay, she shouldn't be wearing that, but c'mon, buddy—just look in a different direction. What's the problem?*

The problem is that as soon as a man is confronted by one sexual image, his brain can start to remember others he's seen.

Gut-Level Memories Are Stored and Replayed

In order to understand this reality, let me (Shaunti) briefly explain something about how the brain amplifies strong memories and then triggers them—in both men and women. You can read more about this in the excellent book *His Brain, Her Brain,* by Walt and Barb Larimore.[14]

Brain scientists have identified a sort of shortcut in which certain memories can entirely bypass the thinking centers of the brain. A powerful emotion-processing area of the brain, the amygdala, acts as a kind of holding tank for impressions and memories that are tied to gut-level responses (such as, for a guy, visual ones). These memories can come back in three different ways: we can recall them on purpose, something can trigger them, or this type of memory can pop up unbidden. Neuroscientists have found that these specific memories can bypass the thinking centers to *involuntarily* pop back up in a person's mind.[15]

We all know what it feels like to specifically recall a memory, so let's examine what happens when those memories are triggered, as well as take a look at those involuntary pop-ups.

Triggers

For women, because we are created to more readily process emotion, those gut-level impressions and memories are much more likely to be *feelings*. For example, you can remember with excruciating clarity what it felt like last year when one of the other moms in your playgroup said something derisive about you in front of everyone else, or how shocked and betrayed you felt when your husband took his mom's side in an argument.

Without our wanting it, the memory of that feeling can trigger others. As you remember when your husband took his mom's side in the argument, you start to think of how upset you were yesterday when you told the kids they were not allowed to watch television until they finished their homework, then half an hour later your husband told them, "Oh, sure, take a TV break."

Even as I'm writing this, I'm getting agitated on your behalf, even though it is a fictional scenario! And I find myself wanting to remember things my husband, Jeff, has done that have upset me, undercut me, or hurt my feelings. I have to work to bring those feelings under control and stop them from taking root. Then I have to choose to put positive feelings and memories in their place.

That is exactly what it is like for men when it comes to visual images and memories. Whereas women's memories are tied more to what they have felt, men's memories are tied more to what they have seen. Their memories are like photographs or videos stored on a computer, and when one photo is pulled up, it can start the whole slideshow.

So let's now go back to that church scenario. Can you understand a little more why the sight of that one woman in the low-cut top would be a problem for the pastor or other males in the church? He sees her—and he doesn't just see *her*. His brain wants to start a parade of other sensual images he's seen, and he has to work to bring those memories under control and stop them from taking root. He has to work to put other honorable memories in their place.

My *For Young Women Only* coauthor, Lisa Rice, and I recorded video footage of teenage guys explaining what it is like to live with a visual brain, which we usually show when either of us speaks at a youth event. In one of the videos, here's how one teenage boy described the conflict he has when he sees a girl at school who dresses to emphasize her good figure and show some skin:

> I try to, you know, [he puts his hands up by his head as if to physically turn it] *rip* my head away from staring at that and focus on what I need to. But a lot of times it is really hard, because if I don't force myself to pay attention, I am going to find myself wandering back there and staring uncontrollably.
>
> It definitely affects the way I operate all day. I'll try and think about other things to take my mind off it. I'll think about cars or, you know, when I'm going to get my baseball bat that is supposed to be coming in the mail . . . something I want to look forward to. But [her presence] is always in the back of my mind, and it is something I can't get out of my head.

And imagine doing that multiple times a day, every day. But most men (or boys) don't want to have to do it in the first place! A guy wants to be able to sit at his desk at work or at school and be able to work . . . or worship God on a Sunday morning . . . or walk down the street thinking about his wife . . . without this constant effort to avoid the triggers, and to not let them send his mind to places he doesn't want to go. And yet, in this culture, constant vigilance is required.

Not only to honor women, by the way, but simply to get stuff done.

When I (Shaunti) was doing my study for *The Male Factor* of how men think in the workplace, this was overwhelmingly mentioned by men of every age, industry, and professional level. It turns out that when a man is confronted by a visual sexual trigger (for example, the low-cut blouse), all the effort he puts into honoring that woman and not letting his mind go in a sexual direction cancels out his ability to concentrate on other things—like what the woman is saying! We heard this so often, I did an experiment and discovered that in a random test the percentage of men who remembered the four points in a ninety-second video dropped by 25 percent if they saw cleavage.[16] In other words: cleavage impairs hearing.

All of this is why I (Craig) can tell you that guys are usually pretty grateful to see a woman dress in a way that is stylish but that doesn't draw overt attention to her body: it means she has made it a nonissue, so the trigger just isn't there. For example, remember our story in the first chapter where Jack talked to Dionne, the financial officer? She's extremely attractive, but because she isn't dressing in neon signs that read "Look here! Look at my body!" he doesn't.

Involuntary Pop-Ups

If you have ever been going about your day and found yourself suddenly worrying about whether your son's fever has gone down, whether your boss liked the project you just turned in, or whether your husband will still be upset about the scratched car, you have experienced the involuntary pop-up memories that the neuroscientists are talking about. They don't have to be triggered by something. Sometimes they arrive spontaneously.

The same is true for men, but because their gut-level memories are more likely to be visual, what pops back up isn't any kind of emotion but rather the mental equivalent of a photograph or a video. It plays across the screen of his mind of its own accord.

This sounds really odd to women. Even weirder, men have no idea that most women *don't* have the same type of sensual visual memories that arrive out of nowhere.

Many years ago, Jeff and I were discussing what I was learning as I interviewed men about this visual subject, and how shocked I was at some of the things they were describing. Jeff was puzzled about why I was so surprised. I shared the resulting conversation in *For Women Only,* but I'll reproduce it here:

JEFF: But you knew men are visual, right?

ME: Well, yes, of course. But since most women aren't, I just didn't get it. I just don't experience things the same way you do.

JEFF: See, I'm not sure I really believe that.

ME: Well, it's true!

JEFF: Maybe we just use different language to describe it. For example, think of a movie star that you find physically attractive—Tom Cruise, say. After we've seen one of his movies, how many times will that attractive image rise up in your mind the next day?

ME: Never.

JEFF: I must not be explaining myself correctly. I mean, how

many times will a thought of what he looked like with his
shirt off just sort of pop up in your head?

ME: Never.

JEFF: Never as in *never*?

ME: Zero times. It just doesn't happen.

JEFF (after a long pause): Wow.

The funniest part was that Jeff didn't really believe me. He told
me later that he just assumed I was embarrassed to admit that I had
pictures of Tom Cruise in my head. It wasn't until years later when
he watched as I shared that story at a women's event—and saw most
of them say "never" right along with me—that he saw how differently men and women are wired.

That is also when he began to understand that many women and
girls truly don't understand what goes through a man's brain when he
sees a provocative image. In fact, a typical man has no idea that during the day his wife (if she is like most women) does not find herself
suddenly fantasizing about him with his clothes off. (And to be honest, most men are quite disappointed when they learn that truth.)

Which brings us to the most challenging thing to understand
about a man's visual temptation.

What He's Actually Tempted to Think

There's no way to sugarcoat this. When that man sees the woman at
his office with her blouse unbuttoned down to *there,* or the teenage
boy sees the girl at his school in the short shorts, the guy is tempted
to picture *all* of her figure.

With no clothes on.

At all.

It doesn't mean he indeed lets his mind wander in that direction—some guys will and some won't—but he's biologically tempted to mentally undress her. In our *For Young Women Only* survey, 85 percent of teenage boys admitted to that temptation.

The next temptation is to savor that image in privacy somewhere and to, well, self-stimulate. (How's that for a euphemism? We'll talk more about this topic in the FAQ section.)

Again, some guys will and some won't, but the temptation is fairly universal and requires a lot of self-discipline to confront. Whether he gives in to this temptation depends to some degree on what his life is like. For example, whether he's married and, if so, whether he knows that his wife desires him and welcomes his advances.

After all, think about what it must be like for a guy to live in today's culture, which provides a near-constant state of sexual stimulation. Consider how much a man would want to know that he could go to his wife in a healthy way, seek that pleasure and that release, and strengthen his bond with her rather than feeling trapped in a choice between constant, frustrating stimulation with no healthy outlet or doing it himself and then suffering the resulting shame and guilt.

Think also about how easy it must be for guys to grow weary of the struggle to keep temptation at bay, to become trapped in those visual temptations and not know how to get free. That is something we will be covering in later sections of this book.

Men Think There Is Only One Reason a Woman Would Dress "That Way"

Because most men have no idea that women don't see the world in the same way, they assume that when a woman views an attractive member of the opposite sex, her mental response is the same as theirs. They assume, therefore, that a woman or a teenage girl who is dressing to call attention to her body knows the exact impact she is having on the men and boys around her. Thus, they think she's doing it on purpose. In other words, in their minds there's only one reason why she dresses that way: she *wants* the guys around her to fantasize about her naked.

I (Craig) can assure you of this. When we see the girl in the string bikini on the beach, the hot twenty-something in the miniskirt at the grocery store, or the woman showing cleavage at the office, we usually assume there is only one reason why: that girl or woman wants men to approach her sexually or fantasize about her sexually. She is advertising.

Now, Shaunti tells me that most girls and women are actually horrified at this idea, and while I know she's not going to lie to me about that, I still have a tough time believing it. But apparently it's true. In her surveys of women and teenage girls, she found that very few of them had any intention of tempting a guy to think or act sexually. Instead, these women said they simply wanted to feel confident about themselves, feel attractive, or wear what is in style. In other words, women and girls like getting attention, but they don't realize that attention isn't at all the type they want.

Many Men Wish They Could Turn Off This Temptation

As you can imagine, many men wish this culture wasn't so visually tempting. But of course other men don't mind the constant stimulation. When the visual memories are triggered, some are perfectly fine with starting a mental parade and letting their brain go in every direction it wants to go. They are fine with indulging in pornography and telling themselves (and maybe their wives) that that is normal and okay.

But many men want to be honorable. We can no longer count the number of men who have echoed this comment from one man:

> If we could, most guys would get rid of this temptation in a
> heartbeat. Although all of us enjoy this aspect of our nature
> when we are alone with our wives, almost every single one of
> my friends hates that we can't just switch it off in public. We
> talk about how we wish we had magic sunglasses that could
> block out those sights the way sunglasses block the UV rays
> of the sun.

Men and boys who try to keep their thought lives pure do not want to have this temptation thrust at them every day, many times a day. I (Craig) can assure you that we come up with all sorts of coping mechanisms to distract ourselves or turn our eyes or thoughts away, but it takes daily vigilance. We would much prefer to not have to deal with it. Unfortunately, that is just not a realistic option.

So instead of focusing only on what can't be changed, let's talk about what can be. Our goal in this book is that you not only understand the men and boys in your life but that you also know how to *support* them, rather than thinking they are weird or withdrawing from them in confusion and adding to the immense pressure they already face.

A man's eyes are one of the gateways to his emotions.

Most of us want the women in our lives to understand how we are wired because it isn't just a clinical, technical thing. As we'll discuss shortly, a man's eyes are one of the gateways to his emotions. The connection between his eyes and his heart is quick and powerful. The things a man sees can actually impact the storage vault of his heart and mind—either in ways that beautifully stir his heart or that create emotional turmoil. Either outcome affects both the men themselves and those around them. This is what we'll examine in the next chapter.

4

The Internal Outcome of External Attraction

I t makes a great deal of difference once women see that there is actually an emotional impact of this physical temptation.

I (Shaunti) once had a friend tell me, with a catch in her voice, "I don't understand why my husband can't just *stop* it." She and her husband were in their late twenties and had been married only two years, but they were in the middle of serious marriage intervention due to her husband's porn problem. He had explained before they got engaged that this was something he was ashamed of and wrestled with, but she didn't fully understand what a hold it had on him. She assumed that once they were married their sexual relationship would fill him up and that he would have no need to look at porn.

"He stopped for a while, but a couple of months ago his computer crashed and he confessed it might have picked up a virus from a porn site he had been on." She looked down at the table where we were sitting, unable to look me in the eye. "He confessed he had been back into looking at things. And our marriage counseling doesn't seem to be helping. I don't understand! We have a decent sex life; I try to keep myself in shape. *Why can't he just not look at those awful websites?*"

Her cry is the same as that of many women who might understand the brain wiring of their husbands and how it plays out but don't understand the emotional issues at play and thus assume they aren't "enough" for their men. Likewise, moms often don't grasp how deep the pull can go for their sons.

Feeling Like a Man

As we said in the last chapter, a man can be (and usually is) attracted to an image without being emotionally attracted to that person. But this doesn't mean that his visual experience has no emotions attached. It does. It is just that those emotions focus inward—not on her, but on *him*.

As a boy or a man looks at an image of a scantily dressed woman, and as all that activity happens in his brain, some powerful feelings are stirred up. Not *memories* of feelings (as a woman might have), but *current* feelings: Looking at that image makes him feel powerful. Desirable. Like a man.

And one reason those feelings are so seductive is that they soothe a hidden and painful self-doubt that most men have, but that most women don't know is there. Contrary to what I (Shaunti) used to think, men hide a great deal of painful self-doubt behind their confident exterior.

You know how as a woman, you have a little voice deep down inside you that sometimes wonders, *Am I lovable? Am I special? Am I beautiful?* Well, men have deep questions too, just different ones.

Their thoughts sound more like, *Am I any good at being a husband? Do I measure up?* A man deeply wants and needs to feel appreciated, respected, and capable. He wants to be good at what he sets out to do as a husband, boyfriend, student, salesman, friend, and so on—but isn't sure he knows how. All too often, in fact, he feels like an imposter. So always in the back of his mind is a very real insecurity that someone's going to find out he isn't sure of what he's doing. About 75 percent of men on my surveys felt this way. They said they worry that they don't measure up . . . that they are inadequate . . . or, worst of all, that the most important people in their lives will look at what they do and say it isn't good enough.

> Men hide a great deal of painful self-doubt behind their confident exterior.

Feeling inadequate or like an imposter is a very male worry and is as painful to them as feeling unloved is to a woman. Yet, as I cover in *For Women Only,* some things have the power to soothe that worry. When you notice what your husband does and thank him for it ("You are so sweet for noticing that we were low on milk and going to the grocery store early, so I didn't have to"), he feels that he does measure up. And similarly, when you and your husband go to bed at night, and you reach for him and show him that you want him sexually, he feels that he *is* worth affirming, that he *is* the desirable man he wants to be for you.

Furthermore, the next day, when he remembers that image of you in bed, he relives the experience—which further reinforces his confidence.

The memory of the image of you desiring him is an amazing, confidence-building feeling for any husband. The problem, of course, is that seeing any sensual image can have a similar effect. It won't be as strong or as meaningful as the sight or memory of you as his wife, but there's still an internal impact that makes him feel good since it soothes his painful sense of vulnerability.

And in today's culture, a guy usually feels that insecurity fairly early in life.

Let's look at the progression of how what a boy sees on the outside can stir up some powerful emotional feelings on the inside, and how that changes and deepens as he becomes a man.

Boys Feel Like Men
When Looking at Those Images

Remember in the last chapter we mentioned that even little boys have a physical, pleasurable reaction to seeing pictures of scantily clad women? Well, a few years later, as that little boy begins to grow, something important happens: the *emotional* pleasure he derives from the sight of an attractive female body becomes more mature as well. Here's how one thirty-year-old guy put it:

> I guess I started to notice girls when I was about nine or ten years old. But I wasn't really noticing *girls,* as in the girls in my class. I was noticing my teenage babysitters or their friends. I was noticing their moms. And I was *really* noticing the college girls who worked out in those tight spandex pants. It was all about boobs and hips and curves. And let me tell you . . . something clicks in a boy. It feels amazing. It is intoxicating, so you want more of that feeling. I had never really seen porn—still haven't, actually. I've been really lucky. But it didn't matter. At night, at the age of eleven, I would

still find myself dreaming about what those college girls would look like in the shower!

A boy's visual awakening makes him feel older and secretly powerful; it is a feeling that boys come to associate with feeling like a man. One forty-something man whom we will call Charlie shared a story with us that is highly representative of others we've heard over the years:

> I can remember when I was in fifth grade, there was this one eighteen-year-old girl who used to come to the neighborhood pool with her family. She would wear a bikini, and—whoa. I had never seen anything like her. I was just . . . well . . . [He laughs ruefully.] Let's just say that I realized I could see her lying out on a beach chair from a sort of hidden alley by the snack bar. She would sometimes undo her bikini top when she was lying face down, so she wouldn't get a tan line, I guess. And I *really* wanted to catch a glimpse. My parents never had a talk with me about sex, and I never knew there was a reason to guard my eyes. So I spent a lot of time there that summer, just staring at her and drinking her in.

Now, not every boy takes the actions Charlie did as a child. A given boy's pattern depends a great deal on his life experience, his friends, and how his parents guide him through this part of childhood and adolescence (which we'll cover in chapter 9). And then ultimately, of course, his pattern depends on his choices each day: what he decides to do about his temptation. But just remember that the temptation itself is fairly universal.

Porn Images Target That Feeling

You may wonder why porn, specifically, has such an impact. Why not pictures of half-naked indigenous women in a desert somewhere? Why do men not hunger to sneak a peek at *National Geographic* the same way as *Maxim*?

While any naked image is likely to stir a male brain physically, it is the message of porn that has a strong impact emotionally. A message that brings—no matter how counterfeit—a sense of affirmation.

As one man explained in an interview, "All those women in the men's magazines and porn sites convey one message: 'I want you, and you are the most desirable man in the world.' My wife may be nagging me at home, the kids may be disobedient, and I may be worried about messing up at work, but looking at the woman in that picture makes me feel like a man."

It is also important to realize that there can be a very powerful draw to repeat that sense of feeling like a man—such a powerful draw, in fact, that it becomes a powerful habit.

A Way of Coping

Charlie, the man we mentioned earlier, is actually someone I (Shaunti) met through a group that—like Craig's ministry—helps men escape the trap of sex addiction. Charlie is a mature Christian man, a godly guy who loves his wife and three kids dearly, but he had been struggling with porn for years. Each time he fell, he knew it was wrong and he felt like a total failure. He would cry and ask forgiveness from God, only to repeat the pattern again. And again.

Thankfully, his wife and his church supported his efforts to get help, and when I met him, he was well on his way to overcoming his addiction. (Just like with alcohol- and drug-rehab programs, many sex-addiction programs emphasize that sex addicts are never truly free of temptation and will need to be vigilant for the rest of their lives.)

As to how his addiction started, listen to the second half of Charlie's description of his fifth-grade summer, secretly observing the eighteen-year-old girl at the pool:

> I know a ten-year-old boy spying on a hot teenage girl sounds like a schoolboy crush—but that's not really it. It went deeper than that. I didn't really understand it until I went through this program, but it was a coping thing.
>
> My dad wasn't the nicest man; and that summer, my parents went through a divorce because my dad kept chasing the women he worked with. It was hard, and my dad was angry a lot. So I would go to the pool every day to escape. But I also found that when I hid in that alley and stared at this eighteen-year-old girl or her friends, it made me feel better. I didn't feel like a stupid kid who couldn't do anything right. I felt something else. Something that felt really good. So when things would be bad at home, I wanted to experience that feeling again. And I discovered I could experience it either by looking at that girl or others, or even by remembering what she looked like.
>
> And then about a year later I discovered something else. My friend Brady had an older brother who kept these *Penthouse* magazines under his bed. And one day he showed them to us. And . . . wow. *Naked women.* The feeling I felt then was even better. My imagination about the girls at the pool had been going wild, but these women left nothing to

the imagination. I found a magazine of my own, and when I felt stupid and dumb, I didn't have to remember the images in my head to make me feel better—I could look at these pictures!

This pattern became an ingrained part of my life . . . and I had no idea how much pain I was setting myself up for. When I started going to a Christian fellowship group in college, God showed me that this was wrong, but I just couldn't get free of it until I went through this program.

Charlie's story is a common one for men with a true porn addiction. But this type of background isn't limited to addicts. Most men and boys in modern cultures today are living in a time that confronts them with all sorts of images that provide pleasure and pose a temptation.

Even If He Is Getting Plenty of Sex

And as we've mentioned before, those temptations—and coping mechanisms—can take hold even if the man has an active sex life.

A colleague of mine (Shaunti's) named Michael Todd Wilson, a licensed therapist who runs a professional coaching business called Intentional Hearts, provided a great explanation of why a man with a sexually attentive wife could still be drawn to porn:

The lie is that what I get from my marriage and what I get from porn is the same. And it is not. That is why he can be enraptured with his wife and still be tempted, and stuck in porn. They don't pull from the same place. I think of them as opposites.

Porn is not about intimacy. It is about anti-intimacy. When I move toward my wife, it is about intimacy. When I move toward porn, it is never about intimacy. So the lie some women believe is, "If I fill him up, he won't want porn." But he's not going to porn for intimacy!

As a man, it is when I feel lonely or impotent or powerless or angry that I might be tempted to go to porn as a way of killing that pain and *not* being intimate, because I don't want to be known and vulnerable in that moment. If I am, I will have to grieve and feel. So in that pain I am instinctively looking to get away from those feelings, to get away from intimacy. That is why a woman cannot simply compensate for porn temptation using physical intimacy.

In other words, if he's looking for emotional intimacy and a healthy bonding with his wife instead of all the images around him, then yes, that need can be met in the bedroom. But if he's using porn to avoid emotional intimacy, then sex with his wife is not going to solve that. In fact, the therapists said, he may even avoid sex because it carries the risk of emotional intimacy.

Even If He Is Married to a Supermodel

The emotional aspect of this is why I (Craig) can tell you that even guys who are married to beautiful, seductive women can fall into the trap of pornography or physical affairs: it isn't just his eyes and a pleasurable part of his brain that are being stimulated through porn. These temptations take a guy with a deep insecurity and need for affirmation—which is most of us—and affirm him. They take a guy who feels like a failure as a husband and tell him he's desirable. And they tempt him to dull his pain at the same time. What a double threat!

It has been clear from every study about infidelity that the reasons men have affairs are not purely about sex or how beautiful the other woman is or how plain his wife is. (Remember Tiger Woods's beautiful wife, whom he cheated on?)

Instead, those affairs—whether with a real woman or with an image of one—are usually about affirmation and flattery, soothing his self-doubt and sense of inadequacy (which is the most painful feeling to a man).

It is never an excuse for a man to cheat on his wife (either physically or with an image), but every man understands the dynamic: when a guy has a wife at home who constantly tells him what to do (implying he has no judgment), who is regularly critical ("I can't believe you let the kids wear *that*"), or who shows that he is undesirable by having little interest in sex, he goes through life feeling terrible about himself. And then, suddenly, there's this woman at the office who tells him he handled that deal so well . . . that he's really good at managing people . . . that she admires him.

Again, there is no excuse for poor choices, but these are often the situations we observe where temptation trumps good judgment.

Bottom line? Complete, nonjudgmental affirmation is powerful for a man. He may not feel like he is getting that from a real person, but he might get that from an image. And to the degree that he is vulnerable, that feeling—however counterfeit—can be very appealing.

The good news, though, is the true, sincere, noncounterfeit affirmation is even more appealing! In my (Shaunti's) research, countless men have told me that they only shy away from true intimacy and vulnerability because they are fearful of getting hurt. But when a man sees that a woman is safe to trust with his tender heart, it is not only a pleasure but an overwhelming *relief* to have a stalwart companion who sees his weaknesses . . . and believes in him anyway. That man, perhaps for the first time in his life, instinctively wants to have someone with whom he can be fully vulnerable and real.

All of this means that true affirmation and compassion help to weaken and break the lure of pornography. Not long ago, a middle-aged man who ran the marriage ministry at his church invited Jeff and me (Shaunti) to speak at a marriage conference. The man described how, fifteen years earlier, he had felt on top of the world—until his business crashed, he and his wife lost everything, and he felt like an utter failure. He secretly turned to porn to soothe the hurt, and it took hold of him for years. But then after ten years, something changed. He realized he needed to confess his problem to his wife. "So," he told us, "being the coward I am, I told her about it when we were praying in church one day. I figured she couldn't kill me in the middle of all those people."

She was hurt and furious that he'd essentially lied to her for so long by not sharing that he had this huge problem. But she said, "Then I realized that there had to be a reason this great man was lying to me. He felt too ashamed, too powerless, or he didn't know how I would react. I was still hurt, but I kept going to God and asking Him to help me forgive my husband and support him in the way he clearly needed."

Even though hurt, she realized her husband needed not just support, but also affirmation. Not for the poor choices, of course, but for the other things he did that were worthy of praise. She gradually

> True affirmation and compassion help to weaken and break the lure of pornography.

developed a habit of telling him those things instead of assuming that he knew how she felt. She thanked him for being a great dad or told him how proud she was of how he handled a business deal. She also told him that as hard as his confession had been to hear, she was glad he had told her—and that she understood how much courage it took for him to do so.

And with that and her prayer support, things inside him changed.

Although it was a hard road, he overcame his addiction. He soberly hastens to tell me, "I have heard that some men have been completely delivered.[17] In my case, I feel more like God has given me the support and prayers of my wife and accountability partners in order to stay free of it. But the temptation itself never fully goes away. I'm like an alcoholic who knows I can never open the door to just that one drink. But as long as I keep that door firmly closed, by the grace of God, it is easier to keep it closed."

And just as with alcohol, drug, or food temptation, there is another clear truth about visual temptation that we've seen in the research: different men and different boys will have very different degrees of vulnerability, curiosity, and strength or weakness in this area. That means it is important to *not* assume the worst (or the best) but to be willing and able to understand where each individual person is in his journey.

5

Different Men, Different Draw

There is a spectrum when it comes to just about everything, and the visual nature of men is no exception. We know that extremes exist and make for great stories, so those wind up being what we hear about most. After all, who wants to read about a bunch of normal people, right? Tell us about the weirdos!

As you're reading along, you may be worried that the man in your life—your son or your husband—is near one extreme and is just one glance away from full-blown addiction. Or perhaps you're reading this and feeling confident that the man or boy you love is on the other side of the spectrum, and you're convinced that this simply doesn't apply to your husband or your son. Maybe you think they are perfectly pure, unsullied angels who have never even been tempted to look sideways at the woman with the boobs hanging out of her dress.

But the truth for the vast majority of men probably lies somewhere in between those two extremes.

Are there men in this world who can view stimulating material, even all the way up to and including pornography, and have it bounce harmlessly off them as if they possess some kind of superpower? Yes. But, just like superheroes, those men are so rare they might as well be theoretical.

What about the other side? Are there men in this world who are so overwhelmingly addicted that every alluring billboard, Victoria's Secret catalog, or sensual beer commercial triggers marathon sessions of porn usage or illicit, emotionally empty hookups? Yes. Those men exist, but they are so rare, you'll likely never know any of them.

Here's what kind of guy you probably know. We can't say for sure, but we can guess: he's a guy who finds some degree of pleasure through some form of visual stimulation. Maybe it's exposed skin, the hint of a bra strap, or a plunging neckline; maybe it's a dress that covers everything but is so tight that it accentuates every curve of a woman's body; or maybe it is even a sexual phrase that stirs up visual curiosity. And whatever it is, the spectrum of response to those visuals is very wide, and he could be anywhere along it.

Let me (Craig) give a real-life sort of example of how different men at different places on the spectrum might react differently to visual images.

I have online alerts set up that will send me an e-mail anytime our XXXchurch ministry is mentioned in an article, or when certain key words like *porn addiction* appear. I read all these articles, which could be anything from an obscure personal blog to high-traffic outlets like *Vice, Huffington Post, TMZ,* or *The Christian Post.* A lot of times I will read these on my phone and think something is particularly important, so I share the link on Facebook and Twitter.

However, several times, within minutes of my sharing these important articles, my phone blows up with e-mails and comments from really angry people. Apparently the regular-browser version of an article (as opposed to the mobile version I viewed) included inappropriate ads or images, or featured a sidebar with provocative pictures or article titles. The full website featured the same really great content I had seen on my phone . . . but it was saturated in tempting images. So although I would never purposefully link to something that could cause someone to stumble, I was, without realizing it, sending people a link to exactly the sorts of triggers that we've been talking about.

So how differently do diverse men handle the trigger of seeing those unexpected provocative links?

Some men can just shrug it off, resize the browser window so they can no longer see the images, read the article, close the tab, then go on with their day.

Other men might want to read the article but realize that because they will want to look at those images and know that they shouldn't, they decide to close the article without reading it.

Still others might try to read the article but are very distracted the whole time because they know there is an image on the side that they desperately want to click.

Some men might forget the article entirely and just stare at the image of the sexy model.

Still others might in fact do an online search for the name of the model, look at some more images of her, and then close the window before they (in their minds) go too far.

And others might do the same thing but not close the window . . . finding themselves thirty minutes later deep in several other Google searches for images of that person naked or even on full-blown porn sites.

Very, very different levels of temptation and reaction to the *same* brain stimulation.

Every man is in a different place, and we're not going to turn this chapter into a catalog of turnons and fetishes (because that can get really bizarre and gross fairly quickly), but the key is to realize that there is some type of visual stimulation that the men in your life are taking in and responding to in some way.

And what you are probably looking for is how to figure out where your husband, boyfriend, or son might be on the spectrum.

So let's look first at some different categories of temptation, so to speak. These are just guidelines, nothing scientific, but they capture what we have heard from thousands of men and multiple specialized therapists over the years. It is also extremely important to note that

> **D**ifferent men will have very, very different levels of temptation and reaction to the *same* brain stimulation.

men and boys in most of these categories simply have the ability to appreciate and even be fascinated by a woman's beauty and femininity (as long as she is not overtly sexual about it) without being caught up in sexual thoughts or temptation. Even if a woman already knows that her man has some sort of an issue here, it is vital to not always assume the worst about him.

This brings us to a critical warning: It is essential that you *not talk to your husband about these categories in any way until you read the rest of the book.* We are sharing these here over the initial objections of several experienced therapists who were worried, as one put it, "You know that there will be many a wife who immediately jumps to categorize her husband so she knows how big of a whip to use on him!"

We were concerned about that, too, but we (and eventually the therapists) realized it was far more important to show you just how broad the spectrum is, then trust you to handle your newfound knowledge well.

General Categories

The Curious Innocent

"The Curious Innocent" comprises many boys. This is the transitional time of life, where all males start to ask that "What's under there?" question. It's the boy who gives sidelong glances at toned bodies almost without realizing it, or the adolescent who notices all things female and begins to realize those visual stimulants create feelings within him that he may not know how to handle.

For example, when my (Shaunti's) son was seven, we were watching a youth-appropriate movie with a scene where a teenage girl lost a bet with a group of other teenage girls and, as a result, had to go skinny-dipping. The scene was tastefully handled, showing a close-up on the actress's face and shoulders as she came out of the water, shivering. However, my son sidled up to the screen, adjusting the angle of his line of sight so that he could (he hoped) look at what was below the picture on the screen. My husband said, "Buddy, I know what you're trying to do, and it won't work." My little boy sheepishly responded, "I was just curious."

The Disciplined Realist

"The Disciplined Realist" comprises many men and some teenage boys. This is the man or boy who appreciates the female figure walking by in the form-fitting workout leggings and either consciously or subconsciously agrees *Yes, she is smokin' hot* but doesn't get caught up in lustful thoughts because of it. He may be frustrated that today's visual temptations exist, but he is pragmatic enough to know that since they aren't going away, he has to train his response to them. So he has become disciplined enough that he can usually look away, take his thoughts captive, or otherwise prevent a slippery slope of internal struggle and greater temptation.

That doesn't mean it is always easy or that he is perfect (even a disciplined man may occasionally sneak a second look), but that he generally has a healthy response to temptation instead of one that is lustful, lazy, or undisciplined.

For readers of faith, you should know that most committed Christian men would fall into this category, especially if they have practiced good visual habits most of their lives. As many dozens of men have told us, "The more you practice discipline, the easier and easier it becomes." (It doesn't, however, mean that many committed Christian men won't fall into other categories; even the most well-meaning, godly guys can find themselves in difficulty in this culture.) This category also often includes middle-aged or older men who find that temptation diminishes as they age.

> "The more you practice discipline, the easier and easier it becomes."

In my (Craig's) experience, our ministry has seen that whereas Christian men are more likely to be Disciplined Realists, the Intense Resisters and Repeat Indulgers tend to be men who are not as driven by a strong faith ideology. (We will look at them next.)

The Intense Resister

"The Intense Resister" comprises some men and many teenage boys. These are the guys whose testosterone is flowing so strongly that they swat down many sexual thoughts from visual temptations during the day. It is an active effort, which in time may become easier as a disciplined habit is built. The intensity of the struggle may be strongest for teenage boys and recovering sex/porn addicts.

In a conversation with Dr. Michael Sytsma, a highly regarded therapist specializing in sex therapy and sexual addictions, he emphasized that these men and boys are often resisting these temptations out of a desire to move toward the disciplined state. This is important, because as Dr. Sytsma put it, "You don't want him to be like an alcoholic who white-knuckles it through his entire life trying to avoid a drink. If a man is coming from being an actual sex addict, he may spend several months as a full-blown resister, but over the long term you don't want him to shut himself down sexually; you want him to enjoy a healthy relationship in his marriage."[18]

The Repeat Indulger

"The Repeat Indulger" comprises many men and most teenage boys. These are males who, like the Intense Resister, are dealing with this intense temptation throughout the day but, unlike him, are not resisting, not handling it well, don't know how to handle it well, or are simply being lazy and giving their thoughts free rein to go wherever they want to go. These are the men and boys who lap up visual stimulation and indulge in the wayward thoughts that come from it, perhaps with not even a concept of why one would want to discipline or train those thoughts in a different direction. The Repeat Indulger is a pivot point; men can tilt from here either back to the Intense Resister or forward to full-blown addiction if they do not change course.

With regard to the sidebar pictures story I shared earlier in the chapter, this is the man who ignored the article and spent time gazing at the picture of the model. As a result, when he sees a sexually stimulating image, he likely doesn't pull back the fantasies that arise but instead allows his thoughts to go wherever they want to go. In many ways, he also doesn't see or honor the woman or the girl as a real person but simply drinks in the sensuality of her body parts.

Dr. Sytsma also noted, "Most teen boys will be in this category simply because they don't know any other way to be at that point. Certainly, some are already trying to learn discipline. But for most, if the boy sees the girl in the short shorts drop something and bend over to pick it up, he probably is going to look. He doesn't necessarily have the skills yet to look away and know what to do with his thoughts instead. He needs to learn that, and to the degree he does, he will spare himself a lot of pain."

The Full-Blown Addict

"The Full-Blown Addict" comprises a smaller number of men and teenage boys. This is the guy who, no doubt about it, is addicted. He might or might not want to change, but regardless of his desires, his thought life and his actions are trapped in a host of unhealthy sexual desires and actions, actions that could end up going far past porn use and into strip club visits, affairs, and beyond. It doesn't mean that an addict goes further than porn use (many men don't) or that such a man can't break free (many men do), but at the moment he is truly in the grip of addiction.

Before You Try to Label Your Man

Before we give some starting points for understanding where your husband or son is on the spectrum, here are two critical cautions.

The first, and most important, caution is this: don't try to figure this out unless you can do it in a healthy way, as a supporter and cheerleader, rather than as a monitor and detective looking for wrong-doing. It would be extremely dangerous to your relationship for you to constantly keep an eagle eye out for any misbehavior on his part. Every now and then we get messages from women who clearly have developed a damaging preoccupation of their own. Here is one such e-mail I (Shaunti) recently received:

> My husband admits he likes to look, and that he needs to control it better by doing more to take that thought captive to the obedience of Christ. He gets the need not to look, but sometimes I notice him still doing it. To be honest, I find myself consumed with this when we watch television or go to a place where there are a lot of people. Most times I purposely look for pretty girls when we are out, or try to notice them as they walk by, then quickly look at my husband to see if he is looking at them longer than he should. Sometimes I say something; sometimes I don't. But it's exhausting.
>
> Sometimes I make comments like, "Really, baby, you had to stay on that channel for that long? Was that appropriate?" Or, "I see you staring at women, and it's not right, and it makes me feel horrible." I just cannot understand why if he is such a strong Christian man, I am not good enough for him. I wonder if he is going to cheat on me. And it is consuming my thoughts.

Can you see how that sort of suspicion and interrogation would hurt your relationship just as much or more than any temptation on his part? So wait to address this issue until you know you won't make the same mistake.

The second caution is this: if you think it's likely that the man in your life has some degree of real struggle, and your conversations with him have confirmed it, you need to go through a process to get him help that makes sure you are *not* the primary accountability partner. That person must be male. You can support, discuss, encourage, and ask questions. But as one counselor put it, "It is destructive if the wife becomes the police. Men don't need a critic but an encourager."

> **D**on't try to figure this out unless you can do it in a healthy way, as a supporter and cheerleader, rather than as a monitor and detective.

So how do you understand where your loved ones are and how to support them? You can pay attention without being suspicious and attacking. You can listen and encourage and support. And you can intervene, *only if and when necessary.*

How Can I Tell Where He Is?

Here are a few steps to consider, after—and only after—you have finished the book and have a more informed and developed understanding of the big picture.

Don't Make Him Pick a Category! (Resolve to Be Safe)

First, approach this in the same way you would want him to approach you in any emotionally sensitive situation. For example, what if he was worried you might be addicted to food? He would know you might be jumpy and sensitive, so he would need to stay calm, understanding, and even lighthearted where appropriate. If at all possible, he would be careful to not cause you pain. He would want to show you that he was empathetic and that it was safe to talk about the issue candidly and constructively.

In the same way, when you eventually talk to your man about this topic, if you handle it in the right way, he is far more likely to be willing to have an ongoing conversation with you, sharing candidly and constructively. That will be a good thing for both of you.

And that means not cornering him.

So when you do talk to him, start with this most important mandate: *do not make him pick the category that he is in.* Yes, we provided the list for you, and it might be tempting to ask your man to place himself on the spectrum. But I (Craig) can almost guarantee that if you share it with your husband or boyfriend, he is going to have a hard time—at least during your early conversations—feeling free enough to honestly put himself in the category that best represents him. Or he may simply struggle with being honest with himself. It may have absolutely nothing to do with you or his trust in you.

Either way, it means that the onus is really on you to determine this yourself by watching and listening. So resolve to listen in a spirit of understanding, without condemnation, and out of nothing more than a desire to love and support him in the way he (and your relationship) needs.

Pay Attention for a Few Days

Now you can start paying attention to your husband, boyfriend, or son for a few days. Not a few weeks, but a few days. Unless you are doing this as part of a formal support process set up because there is an actual problem, set yourself a time limit to pay attention to this, then let it go.

Again, this attentiveness cannot be with a suspicious eye or a desire to monitor him, but because you want to develop an almost clinical understanding of the gears that are whirring in his head when he is around a visual trigger.

So to get that clinical understanding, watch his eyes. Watch his body language. Look at his facial expressions. Where do his eyes land? How long do they stay there? Does he try to turn his eyes away? How many visual triggers confront him that he *doesn't* look at? The latter two questions are just as important to acknowledge and understand.

By paying attention to these things for a few days, your own eyes will be opened and your understanding ignited.

The goal here is not to pounce on him or catch him in the act. The goal is simply to observe and understand how his mind works and what's going on with the man or boy you love.

The goal is also to understand accurately, rather than allow a dangerous misunderstanding. As one specialized counselor put it, "Your task is to *observe* and not *interpret*. Don't start thinking, *He looks at women with big breasts and I don't have them, so he's not satisfied with me.* Because although the reality is that, yes, his brain is fascinated with breasts, he likes his wife's and wants his wife's. It can be so tragically, unnecessarily damaging if she starts comparing herself and creates meaning that likely isn't even there."

Now, all of this can be especially unnerving if you're talking about your son, because that's your sweet little baby! And now, here he is, leering at women! For some moms it is almost easier to think about your husband in this way since you've always known him as a sexual, sensual creature. But coming to terms with your preteen or adolescent son's onset of puberty and sexual awareness may not be nearly as easy. Yet it is an essential part of guiding him into adulthood, especially if you and your husband want to teach him healthy ways to view and treat women.

Start Listening

We are both big advocates of communication since, in my (Craig's) opinion, keeping secrets from the ones we love is almost always dangerous, and learning how to share well is essential. I think we would all live healthier, more productive lives if we learned to be open about who we really are. But communication also must be done to share, understand, support, and build one another up rather than to confront or tear one another down. Yet all too often, when it comes to this issue, those conditions are not met and so fear, not closeness, is the result. As one counselor put it, "There is fear that I don't measure up, fear he is cheating emotionally, fear she will see my struggle, fear she will reject me . . . and on and on."

So if you think there's something more you want to understand, if you want to learn to listen and communicate on this issue, here's what we suggest.

First, remember you should only be coming back to this list for action steps if you've already finished the book. If you haven't yet, do *not* start a conversation or take any other action steps—at all—until you do.

Next, evaluate whether you can even have a conversation with your husband or son. If you don't think there's a big problem, this can be fairly easy *as long as you are curious and supportive and he sees you as such.* Hopefully the two of you are already used to talking openly, even if it isn't necessarily about this issue. If so, then find a good time for a starting-point conversation.

Of course, perhaps there is a bigger issue, or perhaps you suspect one or both of you might have trouble being calm and supportive. And yet even if you aren't comfortable with it, there will be those instances when the conversation must be had. In those cases, it is really important to enlist a mentor, coach, counselor, or therapist to help you have this talk. That idea may seem odd or uncomfortable, but better to bring in someone early than to have to address it in depth later after it has spiraled out of control!

Dr. Michael Sytsma put this in perspective for us as well. He said, "In my experience, fewer than 25 percent of couples in this situation—where there is an issue—could have this type of conversation in a constructive manner, without help. I highly recommend that they stop quickly if it starts to get out of hand and enlist someone to help them have this talk. And if there is a real problem to work through, it needs to be with a truly qualified counselor from the beginning. As some people say, marriages can survive infidelity, but they may not survive bad therapy."

Whether on your own or with someone else helping, the best way to get communication going is to listen. *Really, truly listen.* This is not the kind of argumentative listening where words are coming out of your husband's mouth while you're just waiting for your turn to talk. Or the type of listening that gets easily stung and then sidetracked by hurt feelings when your man reacts defensively and says something harsh.

> **Y**our husband is taking a big risk in opening up his heart to you.

I'm talking about active, compassionate listening: You ponder what your husband is telling you and the fact that he is taking a big risk in opening up his heart to you. Then you mull over his words and consider your own thoughts, not just once but a few times. And then, *before* responding, you repeat back to him what you heard just to make sure you understand what he's saying.

And then you give your opinion. Or explain how you feel.

For the rest of the book, we'll talk a lot about the importance of learning to listen well and being someone who your husband, boyfriend, or son sees as safe to talk to.

If Possible . . . Don't Make the Conversation Too Serious

Something important to remember about tough conversations is this: when you can bring humor into them, or at least acknowledge their awkwardness up front, you can deflate possible tensions before they escalate. So don't be afraid to get goofy or make a lighthearted comment. Yes, this can be a serious topic for both of you. And if things do take a serious turn, you can moderate accordingly, but trust me (Craig): if you want your husband to open up to you, humor and gentleness are great ways to get your foot in the door.

So after you've finished reading the book, make sure you can commit to listening attentively and without jumping to conclusions or judgment. Then, if you want a less-serious approach, show your husband the cover of this book and have him read the following paragraph.

> Hi there! My name is Craig Gross. Your wife is reading this book I wrote about our visual nature as men. We've let her in on the secret that you find looking at women appealing. Don't worry, though: we've explained the fact that God has designed men this way, and that it was intended to be a *good* thing between a husband and his wife—but has sometimes become a difficult thing to manage in today's culture. Your wife wants to understand and support you. I've told her it is probably a good idea for her to talk with you about this. *She promises she's going to listen attentively and without jumping to conclusions or judgment.* So now it's probably a good idea for *you* to talk to *her.* Let her know what's going on in your

mind (she already knows the gist of it—we told her about it).
She wants to know so she can support you in your desire to
honor her and the women around you, so be honest. Even
if you want to be careful about how you word or explain
things, be as open as you can. You know your wife, so you
will know how to share your heart with her.

I hope an approach like this will help if this is a conversation you
need to have with your husband.

Ask questions. Listen to the answers. Try to be lighthearted
where you can. Ask more questions. Unless you're hearing about an
unsuspected true addiction or affair, be willing to smile and joke a bit,
so the whole thing isn't so serious. (We'll be putting more resources,
such as questions you can ask, on our website MenAreVisual.com.)

So that's how to talk with your husband or boyfriend.

What if it's your son? Now that you've had a good conversation
with your husband, let him take the lead in talking with your son,
especially the first time. (And if you're a single mom, don't worry—we
have you covered in a later chapter.) Your husband and son need to
be having regular man-to-man conversations anyway, so this can just
flow right into those as a discussion topic.

Since your husband and your son are both guys, hopefully
they'll be able to talk about anything they need to so that your son
will be able to skillfully navigate this aspect of his nature.

It is important to emphasize: just as with many adult men, be
aware that many young men have been practicing good habits from
the beginning and have truly been able to keep their eyes and
thoughts as pure as this culture will allow. One man I (Shaunti)
know told my husband of something that happened when he sat
down with his nineteen-year-old son to confess a previous challenge

in his own life. He told his son that if he ever had similar struggles he should come to him.

His son looked across at his father and said, "Dad, you need to know: I've never once looked at pornography."

This young man was a freshman in college, and he had never looked at porn. When his dad, stunned, asked how he'd managed to avoid it, the young man said essentially, "From the time I was little, I heard you and other men talk about how dangerous it was, so I had a healthy fear of ever starting down that road. So I never did."

It is so important to be able to be open about this stuff with our sons. So if you're comfortable with it, after Dad has the first conversation, have a deliberately casual and age-appropriate conversation with your son as well. That way, your son knows you are safe to talk to about this stuff if he needs to. The key is this: no matter what he tells you, don't freak out! Keep your face calm, and keep listening.

What Happens When You Listen Well?

When your relationship gets to the point where there are no secrets and no need to hide things, and you feel your spouse understands something that had been very private, something special happens. You feel such a sweet sense of closeness and appreciation for each other. The type of closeness that all of us truly want.

And this can happen with *both* our husbands and our sons, once we learn to share this way.

For example, I (Shaunti) have heard over the years a common story from the women who have read *For Women Only*. A woman would be reading the book in bed, sitting next to her husband, get to a particular passage describing how men think, turn to her husband, and ask, "Is this true?" And a conversation would begin, one that helped the two of them articulate things that perhaps they had never known how to talk about before. "Yes, I had never known how to explain it, but that *is* why I get upset when you say such and such." Or, "Yes, that is how I feel; that's why this particular action means so much to me."

And according to women we spoke to, nowhere was this "Is this true?" dynamic more common than when it came to the topic of the visual nature of men. While some women found that to be a hard conversation, the vast majority reported that they found it a relief to be able to ask questions and prove to their husbands that they were safe to talk to. They were glad to give him an opportunity to talk about something he probably didn't know how to talk about before and to have a chance to begin to understand their husbands better.

Listen to the story one woman told me:

At first, I was so mad to learn how he was wired. See, when we were first married and Jason was trying to explain the visual thing, I would ask, "Have you ever struggled with this?" And he tried to explain that yes, he does at times, but he tries to do the right thing. That he has trained himself to bounce his eyes. Or redirect his thoughts. He was trying to explain it to me, and I didn't get it.

He said, "When I see someone else, I think of you." And I was offended. "I don't want you to look at someone else and think of me!" So I was always looking at him, watching his eyes, and thinking, "Is he looking at that other girl?" It caused a lot of strain.

So here I am years later, reading your book, and at first I was mad. But then I thought, *Wait, this is what he's been trying to tell me for years. Why am I not listening to him?*

So I asked him to explain it again, and to his credit he did, instead of just covering it up because I'd reacted so poorly in the past. And it was really the first time I was willing to truly *listen* to something hard like that, without making him feel awful. It was a real breakthrough for us. I felt like talking about this one issue in a generous, loving way has given us a foundation to be able to talk about *anything* that we need to talk about, without feeling like we have to sweep it under the rug. Not just his stuff, but mine.

It has made us realize: We *can* be honest. We *can* be intimate. We don't have to hide things or hold back to protect ourselves. We can share the real deal and support each other, even when the real deal is sometimes hard. Being able to share everything, and know the other person is safe and able to hear it, has transformed our relationship.

You might think: *Okay, I can see how that would work with a husband or a boyfriend. But what about getting our teenage sons to talk?* You might think that is a lost cause when it comes to any topic, much less a subject as awkward as this. But even though boys use fewer words, many of them will still share things once they feel safe. It is no guarantee, of course, but if you are seen as a good, safe, non-freak-out-mom listener, you might be surprised at how much you hear.

> "I felt like talking about this one issue in a generous, loving way has given us a foundation to be able to talk about *anything* that we need to talk about. It has transformed our relationship."

Of course, some of you are further down the road with this.

You've already had the conversations and unearthed some things you wished you didn't have to hear. So you might be wondering: what happens if you find out that your husband or son has a serious problem related to his visual nature, his actions, and his thought life? We'll go into depth on that in the FAQ section.

And if you're still having trouble with the thought of talking with your husband in a non-knee-jerk way? Well, we're going to cover that next.

6

Nixing the Knee Jerk and Not Missing the Point

So let's acknowledge that for some of us, a knee-jerk reaction is easy, and calm listening is hard. Since the rest of the book is getting ultrapractical—what we actually *do* about everything we've learned up to this point—let's tackle the reality that the key to responding well on the outside is to be careful about how we are responding on the inside. Let's start by sharing three stories.

Story 1

The man came up to me (Shaunti) at my book table after church. The pastor and I had just finished a sermon-series interview about men from *For Women Only,* and the lobby was packed.

"I had to come talk to you." This man looked uncomfortable talking in the large crowd, and I was startled to see that his eyes were red. "My wife read your book, and it has ruined our marriage."

"What?!" I was stunned. *For Women Only* had been out less

than a year, and I had heard many hundreds of stories of marriages saved or restored because wives and husbands were suddenly understanding some deep, hard-to-explain things about each other. This was the first time I had heard the opposite. (Although sadly, it wasn't the last.)

The man looked at the floor. "We had had a good marriage for fifteen years. But three months ago she read that explanation of how men are visual, and it has absolutely thrown her. She says now that she knows men notice other women, she can't trust me anymore. I tell her that I try *not* to notice other women, and work hard to honor God and honor her in my thought life, but it doesn't matter. She can't get over it. She cries all the time and has completely withdrawn from me. She won't make love because she says she is always worrying about what *other* women I am thinking of while we're together. But I don't! I mean, yeah, I have some memories I wish I didn't have, but it's nothing I can't set aside. We have three small kids. I love my wife. And I'm losing her because of this."

I quickly pulled aside one of the pastors of the church. He listened to the man's story, then began a counseling process to try to save the family.

But I was shaken by what seemed like such a destructive overreaction on the part of this man's wife. Especially since the whole point of the book (like its counterpart, *For Men Only*) was to help us understand our mates *so that we can support them* and build better relationships!

It pained me to learn of someone who was not only missing the point of gaining this knowledge but also drastically misunderstanding what we were saying. This wife was so consumed by the misunderstanding that she was unwilling to listen, burying herself in pain, and using her pain as a weapon against her spouse.

Story 2

A while back, I (Craig) met a couple through our website, XXX church.com. The wife in this case clearly had a very different reaction to the revelation that her husband had an actual problem. The husband had been dealing with pornography for many years and had hidden it from his wife. But, of course, she eventually found out.

She didn't know what to do and was so angry that she decided to punish him. She refused to have sex with him anymore. And over the next year and a half, she gained one hundred fifty pounds.

In a joking voice (that I don't think was really joking), she told me, "I showed him."

Story 3

At a women's conference one day, I (Shaunti) told a story about a husband I'd met, who had chosen a very bad response to a depressing situation in his eighteen-year marriage. He shared that he felt his wife spent all her time and attention on the kids, would only have sex with him a few times a year, was often critical of him, and constantly tore him down in front of others.

Then he met a single-again woman while serving on a committee at their church, and that was the beginning of the end. She told him how much she appreciated his work and effort on the committee, affirmed how good he was at this job, and so on. Sadly, despite the fact that he knew it was so wrong, he wound up getting emotionally attached to this woman and left his wife.

Since the women's conference focused solely on women understanding men, I told this story as an extreme example, but one which still carried an important lesson. I said, "There is no *excuse* for this man's actions. But can you *understand* the how indifference, neglect, and outright derision by his wife made the alternative so much more tempting?" I explained that even when we are deeply hurt by a husband's sin, and although the responsibility for his choices lies firmly with him, we should always be willing to look at where God might have us recognize some action or pattern that He also wants *us* to change.

Well. While most of the people in the audience appreciated the challenging point I was making, it didn't go over well with everyone. After the event, two women practically tackled me, furious that I would imply that a woman had *any* responsibility or any need to change herself. They were also spitting mad that I had talked about being aware of our attire, that I would dare to suggest a *woman* might want to change anything because of how *men* think. These two were so furious, in fact, that security had to be called and I was left a bit shaken by the experience.

The Common Thread

What do these stories have in common? They are extreme examples of a common pattern: *someone getting so stuck on a negative knee-jerk reaction to what we're saying that she is missing the main point of what we're saying.* And I (Shaunti) recognize these reactions so well because I, too, initially had some of them when I began learning this stuff!

It is so easy to get caught up in our startled, upset, or indignant reaction to what we are hearing that we don't stop to make sure we are hearing it correctly.

It is so easy to (understandably) focus on *his* responsibilities in these matters that we miss or don't even want to look at the areas where we might have responsibilities too.

It is so easy to want to do what we want to do that we become deaf to the still small voice of God that asks us to lay down our rights, take up our cross (if wearing less-clingy workout pants can be called taking up our cross), and do something we don't want to do purely because it might help someone else. It is so easy to become self-absorbed by some very legitimate hurts that we aren't willing to ask what the other person might actually need from us.

It is so easy to fall into those traps . . . but we can't allow ourselves to. We'll only become defensive, miserable, and so stuck on what *we* should be able to do—or what he should not do—that we're of no use to anyone else.

Are Craig and I saying that we're infallible in our information, or that we're always right in how we suggest that someone handle this issue? Nope. We make mistakes just like everyone else.

But this message is our best effort, after years of research and work in this area of ministry, to accurately portray the visual nature of men *and* to speak to those things women can do to support men. This message also accurately portrays the heart cry of men who want to respect women and who want to keep their thought lives pure in a difficult culture.

Most importantly, it portrays the heart cry of God for us, and what He asks of us, in the Bible—the *whole* of what God asks of *all* of us. Not just the male gender.

You have every right to disagree with what we are saying, shrug, ignore the whole thing, and go your way . . . but we hope you won't do that. We've seen that when women wrestle with anger, indignation, or pain over this message about men, it is often a signal that there is something deeper going on. If this describes how you are feeling, we ask that you think and/or pray through these feelings before you go any further. Seek clarity on your understanding of what we are saying about men, and make sure that you have the right focus on what God might ask of you.

And perhaps you already do. Perhaps you have a clear-eyed understanding and a healthy response to this subject. Even so, don't skip this section. By absorbing these points, you might be able to help another wife, girlfriend, or mom who is wrestling with this topic.

Having a Right Understanding of Men

The woman in Story 1, above, is an extreme example of someone whose misunderstanding of the truth about men caused her to miss the point and react in a way that harmed her husband and her marriage. Craig and I have seen other less-severe misunderstandings that still worry and sadden us:

- "You're saying 'Boys will be boys' and it is just fine for them to indulge in lust!"
- "You're saying men can't help succumbing to their biological urges because they are just wired that way."
- "You're saying women are to blame for a man's wandering eyes because of how they dress."
- "You're saying that women should not be feminine and beautiful."
- "You're saying that looking at porn is natural and acceptable."
- "You're saying that all women are just objects for men to ogle."
- "You're saying I can never match up to the images he looks at and truly desires."

Every one of these comments is not only an inaccurate representation of what we think, but they are the exact *opposite* of what we hold true and say in our ministries. Believing these mistaken conclusions will make it very difficult to have a healthy response to this knowledge. In fact, misinterpretations like these can lead to reactions that cause even bigger problems.

Tellingly, it is very rare that those indignant reactions are from men—at least the men who have actually heard or read what we're saying firsthand. Men tend to get what we're saying and know that our description of their visual nature is the simple truth. And for the most part, they really want their wives or girlfriends to have a right understanding of them and what they face every day.

So if you are indignantly think-ing we are saying "Boys will be boys" or "Women are to blame for men's wandering eyes," then we would like to suggest that you have missed what we have intended to say. Perhaps you skimmed the first half of this book, assuming that you knew what we were going to say.

> If you are thinking we are saying "Boys will be boys" or "Women are to blame for men's wandering eyes," then we would like to suggest that you have missed what we have intended to say.

If you think we're excusing men or blaming women, I would urge you to stop, then pray and ask God to show you what He wants you to see. After that, consider going back and reading portions of the book again.

Having a Right Focus
on What God Might Ask of Us

The second type of angry or indignant reaction we've observed stems from the suggestion that women have any responsibility in the matter:

- "I can hardly write this coherently, I'm so offended at your implication that it is up to us to change what we wear, rather than up to men to change where they look."
- "Why should I have to change what I wear because of *his* problem?"
- "Men are lazy perverts. How dare you put any of the responsibility for their disgusting misbehavior on women."

We said at the beginning that this book was for women, not for men. Our objective is not to help women understand what men should do, but to understand what women can do. Remember, we emphatically believe—and state in our talks and books for men—that *men are the ones responsible for the choices that they make in their thoughts and actions.*

But the only person you can change is the person you see in the mirror every morning. And Jesus was pretty candid about what our focus should always be:

Why do you see the speck that is in your brother's eye, but do not notice the log that is in your own eye?[19]

Yes, the man in your life may need to change as well—even in some pretty major ways!—but Jesus was clear about the order in which *we* should do things:

How can you say to your brother, "Let me take the speck out of your eye," when there is the log in your own eye? You hypocrite, first take the log out of your own eye, and then you will see clearly to take the speck out of your brother's eye.[20]

Certainly, we will be sharing suggestions for how to work with your man on what *he* wants and/or needs to change. But we should always be first asking ourselves, *Am I focusing mostly on what God would have me do, and have I tried as best I can to do it?* This is important not just because it's what God asks but because it's also very practical. Any efforts to jointly discuss your man's actions will bear much more fruit if he sees that you, too, are trying your best to do what God asks of you.

If you are still wrestling with anger or resentment at the idea that women have any reason to change, please realize we've got a lot of ideas for ways to handle things, but every situation is different and we aren't going to make you do anything. What you decide you *will* do is between you and God, and (if you're married) your husband. But the question you need to wrestle with is whether there is something you *should* do. Consider the apostle Paul's message to the church in the ancient city of Philippi:

> We will be sharing suggestions for how your man may want and need to change. But we should always be asking ourselves, *Am I focusing mostly on what God would have me do?*

> Don't look out only for your own interests, but take an interest in others, too. You must have the same attitude that Christ Jesus had. . . . He gave up his divine privileges. . . . He humbled himself in obedience to God.[21]

Ask yourself, *Am I looking out for the interests of others?* For example, are you willing to

- change how you dress if it will help a man who is already struggling to keep his thought life pure?
- adjust your critical voice in your day-to-day life, now that you know how emotionally painful and demeaning it is for your husband or son?
- talk with your man, resolving to be a safe listener so he can share honestly, even if you would prefer to unleash on him for some of his choices?
- set aside your understandable hurt and shame in the face of your husband's or son's poor choices, and ask for help instead of punishing him or hiding the problem out of embarrassment?

Those steps aren't easy. And we wish some of them weren't even necessary. But Jesus gives us a role model to follow in a culture that God never intended to be so difficult.

If you are not a follower of Jesus, then we hope you will see many other reasons to step out and support the men in your life—and men who, in general, want to be men of honor. For example, if you have a son who wants to honor the girls at his school or the women at his office, wouldn't you want *them* to help him do that, instead of thumbing their noses at his efforts and making it more difficult? Or if you think it's just fine to treat your husband a certain way, ask yourself: would you want your son's wife or girlfriend to treat your son that same way?

How to Have the Right Focus

How do you end up with the right understanding and the right focus, especially if you don't really want to?

Ironically, your best tool for having the best reaction to this knowledge is also the best tool for men who are trying to keep their thought lives pure.

When I (Craig) speak to men's groups, I often reference the biblical directive to take every thought captive out of reverence for Christ. But I have come to see that this instruction applies to *everyone*—including women. In this area of ministry we spend a lot of time hammering men to step up to the high calling that God has for them, to realize that Jesus died to set them free from the grip of temptation and sin, and that they *must make the right choices* that will honor God and honor the women around them.

Do you mind if I exhort you just as strongly to honor God and the men around you? Do you mind if I challenge you to take every thought captive too?

Just as men need to ensure they don't let their visuals run away with them, you need to do the same with your thoughts and emotions about what you have just learned. If you are upset by what we're saying, please make sure that your understanding of those facts is accurate.

Or maybe, as we noted, your understanding is completely accurate and you are just angry—angry with God for making men with a visual brain, angry with men for being visual, or angry with us for suggesting that women have a role to play in supporting men. Maybe you just want to toss this book out the window and ignore everything we have said.

But doing that will only lead to more frustration and disappointment. Seriously. Because it would mean trying to contradict the ways God created us to think and function, and instead trying to force everyone to interact with the world in the same way that you do. You can convince yourself that you're right, and men are just wrong, and there's no reason you should have to change anything.

But if you do, I think you will find yourself trapped in a bitter existence.

Or you could be willing to do the opposite. I hope you will do the opposite. I know it can be tough, especially when you are wrestling through new knowledge that might have startled or angered you. But being willing to keep your heart open to what God wants to show you and ask of you will pay off.

Again, the wiring of the male brain *is not an excuse for misbehavior.* All of us are responsible for our own actions and the fallout that comes from disappointing those we love. But when we can know *why* we or others do the things we do or think the things we think, we can get a much better handle on ways to take control of the situations we find ourselves in. We can live the abundant life, in the abundant relationships, God has for us—and that we most want.

Sadly, some men simply won't care about misbehavior or what their responsibilities should be. Those men are probably in the minority, but they do exist. But even in those cases, women are not absolved of the responsibility to keep an open heart that is willing to hear from God, and to handle this subject with the maturity and the others-focused outlook that God asks of us—and that men need as they try to navigate the minefields of this culture.

7

Every Woman's Response

Over the next three chapters, we're going to be gradually narrowing our scope. I (Shaunti) am going to start here with the broadest look at how women and girls can respond to these truths in our day-to-day lives. In the next chapter, we will narrow in to see how someone can respond as a wife, followed by a chapter on how to respond as a mother.

So let's begin here with what God asks of every woman—and every teenage girl—in this exhortation from the apostle Paul to Christians in ancient Rome:

> Therefore let us not pass judgment on one another any
> longer, but rather decide never to put a stumbling block
> or hindrance in the way of a brother.[22]

As you have seen, today's culture can present enormous challenges for our very visual men who want to try to respect women and honor God in their thought lives.

Some women might point out that we cannot cause a man to stumble, because his actions are his responsibility. Very true. But we are fooling ourselves if we think that means we have no responsibility. Let's face the incontrovertible fact: *There are things we can do that will put a stumbling block in the way of a man who wants to honor God.* This means that if we selfishly go right ahead and do them, it is just as much of a sin as if that man were to ogle every woman on the street and lust after her in his heart.

For example, if we decide to flaunt what we've got, knowing what we know now, it is the equivalent of being told that a man is going to be walking down this particular path, then picking up a giant paving stone that we have been told over and over might make him stumble, and deliberately dropping it directly where we know he is about to step. Once we have dropped the stone, we stand back and watch . . . as he trips and maybe falls. Then when he gets up, bruised and bleeding and hanging his head in shame, we stand there with our arms folded and raise our eyebrows and say, "It's his fault."

How dare we treat our brothers in Christ this way?

Do you see why this is such a big deal? If we are not willing to allow our eyes to be opened to our part in this area, we are being deliberately hurtful to men and disobedient to God.

The area that we have the greatest control over is how we dress. We have to decide whether our clothing choices are going to help men who want to honor women, or put a stumbling block in their path. The choice of attire is one that has to be made by every woman, of every age, background, body type, and stature.

I (Shaunti) recently saw a blog called "Modesty, Yoga Pants and 5 Myths You Need to Know," by Phylicia Masonheimer, a young, beautiful newlywed. Phylicia did such a great job of making many of the points I wanted to communicate that I got her permission to include a few of them here.

In response to the common concern that "women are unfairly singled out about their clothing," she explained something that Craig and I have both seen many times:

> It's true, lust is a sin, and men shouldn't entertain it. But the level of their lust is directly related to how much of our bodies is available to lust *after*. The less we advertise, the less opportunity we give them to covet our bodies.
>
> [I mentioned the claim that] women have been unfairly singled out concerning modesty. While men *are* responsible to honor us with their eyes and minds, when we dishonor *ourselves* by what we wear, the real unfairness is to the men.
>
> Do we really expect to wear whatever we want and then tell them not to look at us? Do we really expect to fit in with the latest (often sexually promiscuous) trends and NOT be viewed as an object of sexual desire?
>
> It is not just his job not to look; it is *our responsibility* to provide nothing provocative to look at. We cannot blame men for what we instigate, and it is time for women of God to start acknowledging our responsibility in this matter, taking up our cross, and honoring God with our dress.[23]

When I read that, I wanted to stand up and cheer. And so did many of the hundreds of thousands of other people who have read and shared her blog post. Others have criticized, misunderstood her message, or become indignant that she would dare to tell women they should make any changes. (Hmm. That sounds familiar.)

Christian Men Already Feel Guilt About Their Wiring

Being willing to take responsibility is also important simply to show solidarity with the men in our lives. Especially because many men in this culture already feel guilty just by *existing* with a male brain.

Phylicia made another great point that Craig and I know to be true. Referring to how often people indignantly tell men in the church that they need to do a better job of guarding their eyes and honoring their sisters in Christ by where they look and what they think, Phylicia emphatically agreed that it is vital to address men and the issue of lust. But then she pointed out,

> But the reality is that many Christian men—at least the ones
> who truly seek after God and are convicted by His Spirit—
> are not only *aware* of their lust problem, but guilty about it.
> They are not all shameless beasts looking for an opportunity
> to undress women in their minds.

I would go even further than that. I have now interviewed and surveyed thousands of men. And *most* of them, especially if they are Christian, are already aware of their tendencies and temptations, and—even if they successfully fight them—feel somewhat torn and guilty.

This is especially the case because many guys aren't fully aware that their visual biology, and the temptations that come with it, is anything other than normal. My husband, Jeff, told me very early after *For Women Only* released that he saw an outpouring of relief among men who had read the visual chapter in the book and suddenly realized, *I am not weird.* As he put it,

Guys don't generally sit around and talk about this kind of internal stuff the way women do, so how would they know that other guys are the same as they are? It's not like you sit around at Starbucks going, "You got images?" "Yep, I got images." So some guys have been feeling shame for years because they thought that the *temptation itself* meant that they were failing and sinful.

It is a relief for a man to know that just having an image pop into his head doesn't mean he's a failure. For him to know that "Yeah, I don't like that it confronts me, but what matters is what I do next."

Making Fashion Choices That Respect Men

So how can we make clothing choices that are honoring? Thankfully, being careful doesn't mean being frumpy. You can wear trendy fashions just like everyone else, look confident and beautiful, and make a terrific impression. The key is knowing how to make the impression you *want* to make as opposed to the possible impression that "I want you to fantasize about me in your bedroom later tonight."

Lots of books and websites for girls and women detail everything from modest fashion, to having a great image in business, to how to evaluate all the different elements of your wardrobe. They can give far more specific dos and don'ts than we can get into here. So we're going to concentrate on what we consider the most important things to remember and do based on the most important things we know about men's visual nature.

> The key is knowing how to make the impression you *want* to make.

1. *"With great power comes great responsibility."* Remember those words from Spiderman's Uncle Ben. And in this case, the better a female's figure, the greater the power—as in the power of a magnet. The younger, hotter, or more attractive a girl or a woman is, the more likely her body is to draw a man's eyes, even if she really isn't trying to do so and even if he didn't want to notice.

   It certainly isn't fair, but if you're in the enviable position of having a great body, you'll need to be that much more aware of what you're wearing, to avoid the triggers we talked about in chapter 3.

   It's also worth noting: if you understand the power you have and you decide intentionally to wield that power in order to draw the stares of men, then you should take a long look at that motivation and determine *why*. What needs of your own are you trying to meet? Where are these desires coming from? And how can you fulfill those desires in a healthy way, rather than in a way that says "I don't care if I'm putting the skids under some guy who wants to keep his thought life pure, as long as I get the attention that feels so good"?

2. *Careful of the curves.* When I ask men what it is that has the most magnetic draw for a man—what makes it the hardest *not* to look—the responses I hear most often are "her curves" or "a glimpse of anything that is supposed to be hidden." If you have read this book up to this point, their answers don't surprise you. And many men have mentioned how amazed they are at how many women seem to intentionally choose to *not* cover up

their curves just a bit more. For example, men have mentioned how often women will wear leggings or spandex shorts, without something like a tunic to cover them up. After all, they point out, those outfits hug every curve of a woman's body just as if she were naked—vividly maximizing her assets.

Just remember that emphasizing the curves or showing the hidden things will be tempting—while simply slipping on a jacket over a tight top, wearing a cami under a low-cut shirt, wearing a pair of running shorts over spandex, or putting on a longer top over leggings will make a trigger much less likely.

3. *Examine the extras.* It is amazing how many little triggers can be missed even by a woman who wants to be mindful. I (Craig) am constantly startled at how easy it seems to be for a woman to not notice that her shirt is gaping between buttons in the front. You do know what shows when you turn sideways, right? Or think about what a guy who is taller than you is seeing when he stands beside you and has to look down (like if you're both working on the same papers, for example). It is the same thing that would show if you leaned over in front of the mirror. We have heard fashion consultants say that so many of those little slip-ups can be completely avoided if you do that extra check in the mirror in the morning.

We want to encourage you that many of the changes that would make a huge difference are very small. For example, if your skirt is on the shorter side, be aware of how much it will ride up when you sit down. Or if you wonder *Is this top too clingy?* err on the side of getting a larger size.

I (Craig) know that Shaunti and I are going to get angry e-mails from women saying, "You're telling women they have to wear a potato sack." We are not. Please go back and reread the earlier being-careful-doesn't-mean-being-frumpy-and-you-can-still-dress-fashionably paragraph.

You can still be confident and beautiful, only it will be *you* that the men around you are seeing, and not your . . . well . . . whatever.

The Heart of the Matter

If you are willing to make changes—or at least are trying to be willing!—then we are so grateful. We know that it might not be easy for everyone.

We hope you will not only be willing to do something about it but be willing to say so. To champion care and awareness, and the *why* behind it, in yourself and other women. Because ultimately the issue is not really about modesty. It is not about what we wear. It is about the state of our hearts.

I (Shaunti) was so encouraged by a woman I met recently on an airport tram. She struck up a conversation, then looked chagrinned at my response to her question about what I did for a living. "I've read your book," she said. And when I asked when, she looked embarrassed. "Uh, sort of, two years ago. And then for real a few months ago."

There was clearly a story behind her hesitation, so, amused, I asked what she meant by "sort of."

She looked even more embarrassed. "Well, I threw it in the pool the first time."

I laughed out loud. "I can guess which chapter you were on. The visual chapter?"

"Yes, how did you know?" She started to grin, then explained. "I was sitting by our pool reading it and got so spitting mad that I tossed the whole thing into the pool. Then I fished it out, ruined, and threw it in the trash. My husband just looked at me and didn't say a word. I knew my husband had wrestled with porn here and there, and that it was something he was working on. And I was so mad that you would imply that women had any role to play, or should have to change anything because of *the man's* problem. Oooooh!" I could hear the echo of her anger, still, in the growl in her voice.

A bit tentatively, I asked, "What happened a few months ago?"

"A friend of mine—who didn't know about that little pool incident—gave me a copy of the new edition of the book. My husband and hers were both in the men's group at church, so she knew they were dealing with a few similar things. And she said it had really helped her understand him better. So I started reading it again. And this time, I told God, 'Okay, I still don't like this very much, but I want to hear what You want to tell me.'" She stopped.

"And . . . ?" I prompted.

"And I still didn't like it very much!" She laughed, ruefully. "But I realized that if I cared about my husband, it didn't matter if I didn't *like* the truth; the question was whether it *was* the truth. So I asked my husband to read that chapter and be really honest with me. And he said, yes, every bit of it was the stuff he'd been trying to explain but didn't know how to say."

"How have things been since then?"

"I've seen how much it matters when I am willing to support him more, rather than thinking it is entirely his issue and I can butt out. Or how much it means to him when I am willing to change something I'm about to wear to the office that I know he's uncomfortable with me wearing. I used to think it wasn't his business, and

I made it very clear he wasn't allowed to have an opinion! But truly . . . we're supposed to be one. So *of course* it should be his business."

I know it sounds funny, but I was so proud of this woman, this complete stranger who had had such a negative reaction but was willing to move past that to support her husband in the way he needed.

> "I realized that if I cared about my husband, it didn't matter if I didn't *like* the truth; the question was whether it *was* the truth."

We'll be talking about additional ways we can do that in the next chapter, but in the meantime, here are some closing words for you to think about.

With what I (Craig) and my team do at XXXchurch, it's easy to think we're focused on behavior modification. And while we do care about helping people change their behavior, that isn't our goal. Our goal is to get people to look within themselves and discover *why* they do what they do, then to make healthier choices as a result of that understanding.

In other words, we believe that if you are working on your heart, your behavior will follow suit.

8

The Wife's Response

If you are married, you may or may not want to toss this book into a pool, like the gal in the previous chapter, but you probably have a whole bunch of swirling thoughts and questions. And many of those questions likely center around what you should actually do as a wife or girlfriend. That's what we'll be covering in this chapter.

Because my (Craig's) ministry and expertise is in this area, most of the input and advice from this point on will be from me, but Shaunti will be chiming in too. Here are five big-picture things we suggest.

1. Talk About All of This . . . Calmly

We already began digging into this, but regardless of where your man lands on the spectrum we outlined in chapter 5, this is the starting point: You should probably talk about it. But you also have to decide when and how.

If, after reading through the whole book, you find that you are handling this knowledge well and are not unduly agitated by what you've learned—and if you don't think there is an unusually major issue to address—talking to your husband (or boyfriend) is a good first step since you will be able to talk about it calmly.

But . . .

If you're agitated by what you have learned, or if you think there may be a significant issue requiring outside help, you must think about it and pray about it *before* you talk to him. As mentioned earlier, do not even broach the subject until you can talk about it calmly, then get whatever help you need.

Your husband may or may not even want to talk to you about his visual nature and what this part of his life is like for him. This may be something that he has never shared with anyone before. Or he may wish you understood it but doesn't know how to explain how it is for him. He may be worried that whatever he says will be misunderstood. He may have something he needs to confess to you. Or he may be someone who is not dealing with any real struggles. But one thing is sure: you will never find out what he's truly thinking and feeling—what is actually going on inside of him—if he sees that you are agitated and upset and feel threatened about what you have learned.

Unfortunately, far too many men have learned the hard way that their wives aren't safe to talk with about this, no matter how much they want to.

A few years ago, I (Shaunti) was interviewing a man in a coffee shop near a church where I was speaking. He said, "I saw an announcement in our church bulletin that a pastor was starting a men's group on Saturday mornings to work through the book *Every Man's Battle.* I had been really struggling lately. I had some bad habits and didn't know how to break them. I hadn't known how to talk about it with my wife, Carla, so this gave me the perfect opening. One of my buddies was going too. I casually showed Carla the bulletin and said, 'Hey, Brad is doing this men's group, and I'd like to go to this. I think it would be good for me.'"

His mouth twisted. "But as soon as I brought it up, she panicked. She was like"—his voice rose sharply in imitation of female agitation—"'What are you saying? Are you saying you're attracted to other women? What are you saying?!'"

He held up his hands in surrender. "So of course I said, 'No, no, never mind. It's not a big deal.' And that was that. I would love to talk about this with her. But it's not worth upsetting her like that."

I (Craig) can tell you that we men feel very protective not just of our wives, but also of ourselves. Most of us want to share our lives with our wives. But there are very specific things that will allow us to do that—and some that almost ensure we won't.

So let me share some of those thoughts with you—some ideas that, by the way, will help you talk to your husband about any sensitive issue, not just this one.

Most important: although I can't tell you the exact words to say, I can tell you that taking it all in stride, no matter what comes out of his mouth, will go a long way toward building the kind of trust and rapport you need to have with him. *You are still allowed to have feelings about this,*

> Most of us want to share our lives with our wives. But there are very specific things that will allow us to do that.

but the key is how and when you express those emotions. If your husband has been reluctant to talk about this part of his life, it is extremely important that he sees you as someone he can risk sharing with. That will help keep the door open, no matter what is going on, good or bad. So go into the conversation with a strategy for how you will respond (or not respond) if you hear something upsetting.

In the end, you need to be you and to honor what you feel. My only advice is that you do your best to honor those feelings in the healthiest, most constructive way—in the same way you'd expect your husband to do for you.

If you're not yet married . . . We want to have a quick word with those of you who are dating someone seriously or are even engaged to be married. It is just as important—if not more so—for you to be able to understand where your man is on this issue since you may be evaluating whether or not you should get married to this person. If he is able to talk with you about this openly, that is a good sign. If he seems to be hiding something, be very careful in moving forward in your relationship until you understand what he is cautious about. Is he secretly looking at porn and trying to downplay its severity? Or is he simply just embarrassed about some curiosity he had at the age of fifteen, and the fact that he browsed on the Internet until his mom caught him? Or is he just not used to talking about something like this with a woman instead of with other guys, who all understand the temptation? It is vital to learn whether or not he has a struggle that will affect you in marriage and to be able to talk about this stuff openly.

I (Craig) have been married sixteen years, and I can tell you that what the experts say is true: communication is key to relational success. If you can't learn to talk about tough stuff—and to keep talking—then your relationship is going to suffer. If you can't learn to talk at all, then you're going to have some serious challenges that could truly threaten your relationship. This is something to think about before you take any further steps along this particular relational road.

2. If You're Married, Give Him Positive Visuals of You

Maybe your husband hasn't told you this himself, but I (Craig) can tell you for him: he likes looking at you naked. Yes, even if you've been married for many years and have popped four kids out of that body.

This is the positive, wonderful, awesome part of being a visual guy. A man finds it very enjoyable to have this ability when it is channeled entirely toward his wife. And having the memories of you in all your glory gives him something to think about that honors God and honors you, especially when he is tempted to think about other images. He can switch his thoughts to you instead.

> **H**aving the memories of you in all your glory gives him something to think about that honors God and honors you.

Yes, this is a real thing that men can—and will—do. So, in practicality, here are some ways you can give him healthy, wholesome visual stimulation:

- Have sex with the lights on every now and then; you'd be amazed at how far this will go toward making you his default sexual image.
- Invest in some lingerie—and give him the chance to tell you what he likes.
- Do the best you can to take care of yourself. I'm not saying to work out for two hours a day; just do, literally,

whatever you can. Even if it shows minimal impact. Trust us. The effort *will* be noticed and appreciated. (And yes, maybe your husband should hit the gym with you!)

- Put on a nice dress occasionally to remind him that you are a desirable woman.
- Flirt with him and be sexually playful. Hike up your skirt when no one is looking. Draw his attention to those parts of you he finds attractive.
- Smile.

Take a deep breath. I realize that those small points I just shared could have sparked some serious emotions or resistance. *Sex with the lights on? Forget it.* You don't know how many women I talk to that automatically toss out that idea! But if you understand the visual nature of men, then you'll understand that whether you love your body or not, your husband doesn't like sex in the dark as much as sex with the lights on. He wants to see you. All of you. For some of you, that means coming to terms with your own body and how God made *you* beautiful. The more comfortable you are with yourself, the easier (and more fun!) this will be for you.

Let me explain the lingerie. We live in a world where the Victoria's Secret annual fashion show is on television during prime time and stores like that are in every shopping mall in the country. There is nothing wrong with most of what they sell when put in the proper context of marriage. Your husband is not expecting you to look like a lingerie model, so don't skip over those stores just because you don't look like the girl in the window! Visually, some of that lingerie is such a big turnon for husbands, and your willingness to visually spice things up makes him feel that you care about him. (And just a hint: Most men dislike flannel pj's. We really do.)

3. Help Prevent Some Preventable Problems

Another key way to be a part of supporting your husband is to think of things in your world—the magazines you subscribe to, the media you watch, and so on—that could trigger temptations that he does not want to have. Day-to-day life in every household looks different, so the answers will likely be unique to your family.

For example, let me (Shaunti) share something from my interviews with guys. I'm absolutely astounded at the number of men who have told me that one of the things that trips them up is the temptation that comes from having catalogs from places like Victoria's Secret or Boston Proper delivered to their house every few weeks and sitting out on the island in the kitchen.

Does that describe your situation? If so, this is a toxic temptation for your husband—and in some ways even more for your son! If you have a male of any sort living in your home and you have subscribed to receive any lingerie catalogs or any catalogs that feature lots of sultry-looking women with cleavage down to *there*, well, you'll have to decide what to do about it.

Another thing to consider is what media you ask your husband (or son) to watch with you. We'll talk about watching television and movies with our kids in the next chapter, but in the meantime, consider something pastor Andy Stanley told me (Shaunti) during a pastoral interview on *For Women Only* one Sunday morning in 2004.

> The reason I sometimes don't want to go see the chick flicks
> with my wife isn't that I'd rather see something be blown
> up—although, yes, I would rather see something be blown
> up!—but the reason I don't want to go see all the chick flicks
> is that I don't want the sex scene from *Cold Mountain* in my
> head for the next ten years.

A few months later, Jeff and I shared that comment at a marriage conference in Phoenix, and during a break, a couple walked up to talk to us. Apparently, as soon as I had relayed that comment, the wife had turned to her husband and whispered, "I don't even remember that there was a sex scene in *Cold Mountain*."

Without missing a beat, her husband stared straight ahead and drawled, "Yep."

4. If He's Got a Bad Habit, Expect Him to Work Hard to Change It—and Actively Support Him in Doing So

There are many men who, try as they might, simply have a difficult time completely avoiding pornography. They want to honor their wives, they want to honor God, and yet, as Paul so eloquently put it in his letter to the Romans, "I want to do what is right, but I don't do it."[24] A few of these men are truly lifelong addicts, but most of them aren't—they're just men who struggle with what can occasionally seem like an insurmountable task.

What if you know or love someone like this? What can you do for him? For the rest of this section, we'll give you some starting-point ideas for what you can do. We address a few more in the FAQ section at the end of the book. But in the end, these will only scratch the surface and the specifics will entirely depend on your individual situation. There are whole books and ministries devoted to walking a husband and wife through this in detail (you can find many of them at MenAreVisual.com/resources). So the first and most important suggestion is to seek out those resources, then get whatever degree of aid is needed for your unique situation. Here are a few other steps.

Pray for him—and you. This is not just a token suggestion. You need to pray for your man to be strengthened and equipped to stay pure in a very difficult culture, and for you to have wisdom on what to do along the way as well.

Expect your man or your son to work his hardest to do what is right. God sets the bar high (going so far as to call internal lust an act of adultery), and so should we all.

As he takes whatever actions he needs to take, do your best to be supportive and understanding. Let him see that you are trying to understand *him* even if *you* have been the one hurt. It is natural to ask what a man should do, the techniques he can and should employ, and so on—but that isn't the topic of this book. We must always bring our discussion back to what we as women can do. That said, we do give a few ideas below, in the FAQ section, and on our website, but if there is a real problem, your husband or son needs to be under the guidance of someone who is used to walking men through this so he can implement a well-developed plan.

Encourage your man to be in some kind of accountability relationship with other men. There is no substitute for accountability and support within the context of male bonding, even when a man has no significant issue to address, but it becomes absolutely essential if he does.

I (Craig) don't have hidden issues, and I talk to my wife about everything, and even I have a small group of other men who help keep me on track and whom I, in turn, help. It's just a healthy way to maintain the kind of life I want to have, and I can't recommend it highly enough. You cannot and should not be the only person your husband talks to about these things.

I wrote a book called *Open: What Happens When You Get Real, Get Honest, and Get Accountable* in which I tried to explain why accountability is not just needed but imperative. It is essential.

Many men, though, are instinctively terrified of this kind of vulnerability. They see accountability as a sign of weakness when being open is really a sign of strength.

So do not judge your man if he seems very reluctant. But simply and nonjudgmentally encourage your husband or boyfriend to take the lead in this area with a few close men in his life. Don't force it though! It has to be something he is willing to do *for himself,* or it won't work. So mention it, then ask him what he thinks of the idea. ("I hear that it helps men to hold each other accountable and support one another. What do you think? It would mean a lot to me if you did that.") If he is willing, great. But if he is reluctant, pray that your man sees that he can't and shouldn't live life all alone and that he comes to realize that he needs other people.

> There is no substitute for accountability and support within the context of male bonding, even when a man has no significant issue to address, but it becomes absolutely essential if he does.

It might surprise you relational women, but the number one thing I hear over and over at XXXchurch.com is people (especially the men) telling me they feel like they are alone in their struggles.[25] Once a man realizes he isn't actually alone, a candid and supportive relationship with one or more other guys sometimes becomes more appealing.

Ask him whether there is anything you can do for him. My (Shaunti's) husband asked me a favor when he began working from his solitary basement office at home, rather than from a bustling office with fifty of his employees. He said, "Would you ask me every few weeks, 'Have you been pure?'" He explained that at his company, if he accidentally happened across something on the Internet that was tempting, it was easy to resist because people were always in and out of his office. But alone at home, he wanted the assurance that I would be asking him that question, which would help incentivize him to be able to always answer yes.

Now, before you try to set that up in your life, realize that Jeff and I are a bit unusual, given what we study in our research! Most men will probably not want to have this type of discussion with their wives. And since a man needs a male accountability partner for this stuff, that reaction is fine. It would be demeaning and counterproductive for you to be his accountability partner, since that makes you the police. And it would be unhealthy for you to insist on being updated like that, unless doing so was part of a guided accountability process set up as part of a recovery program.

But the point is that you can ask if there's anything you can do to support him, then see what he says. For example, maybe he's just been dying to ask if the family could cancel its cable subscription, or if you could use the parental controls to block certain channels, just so he knows that he won't be tempted to watch certain shows. Ask. You won't know how you can help until you do.

Make technology work for you. Instead of technology always being something we're fighting, I (Craig) think it is important to enlist it. For example, choose a software package to monitor Internet traffic. Although we are a ministry before we are a software company, XXXchurch created free Internet accountability software called X3watch. The user downloads the software or the app for iOS or Android, and immediately it asks him for two e-mail addresses of accountability partners. Each week those people will get an e-mail detailing any questionable websites that he has tried to access. The process of setting this up opens the door for conversations. We have over a million people using X3watch. It takes courage for people to download this and invite others in to be part of the accountability process. But using this software is one signal that your man is serious about this stuff. In my talking with husbands and wives about these issues, some men choose to have their wife receive their e-mail alert. Other wives I speak with do not want to, or a counselor has advised that this is a situation in which the accountability, for now, primarily needs to rest with other men. I will leave that one to you to have a conversation about with your husband.

5. If He Doesn't Think Looking at Porn (or Staring at Other Women) Is a Big Deal, Seek Help

If your man thinks looking at porn or ogling women isn't a big deal, he is deceived. More importantly, because he is almost certainly entertaining lustful thoughts for women other than you, by Jesus's definition he is probably committing adultery in his heart. But he is also deceived because if it bothers you, it should be a big deal for that reason alone.

Now, let me (Craig) be clear: I'm talking about a guy who is regularly looking at porn, not a man who is visual and experiences the visual temptations of every man in this culture. Not a man who has ever snuck a peek at porn in the past. If your man (or son) says, "Honestly, I am mostly okay with my thought life, and I'm handling the temptations okay, so it is not a big deal," that is different. If he struggles, but is trying to help you understand that his struggle isn't unusual, or that it doesn't affect his love for you, that is different. What we're talking about here is a guy who is purposefully looking at porn on some sort of ongoing basis but completely downplays its significance.

The reality is, when it comes to this particular issue, it doesn't matter if your husband or boyfriend doesn't think looking at porn is a big deal. *If you care about it, then so should he.* And he should do whatever it takes to get it out of his life.

When he is watching porn but tries to tell you it's no big deal, he's actually choosing to indulge in his lusts over honoring your feelings and thoughts. To me that sounds like a symptom of an issue that runs much deeper than simple visual stimulation. And so that is something that he has to be willing to address. If he cares about you, then he should care about your thoughts and feelings on this issue. I have seen so many women be deceived by their husbands into believing that this is not a big deal, then the women begin to view pornography with their husbands. Don't go down this road. You are opening a door that you don't want open. If he doesn't see how this makes you feel and how this hurts you, I would recommend counseling with a professional for the both of you to work through this issue.

Trust God, Even If You're Uncertain Whether You Can Trust Your Husband

So, how are you handling all this new information? Have you been able to go with the flow when it comes to these revelations about your husband (or boyfriend), or has it really thrown you for a loop? If the latter, let us reassure you: you may be reeling a bit, but God is not. God understands this temptation better than we ever could, and if you ask Him, He *will* be guiding your every step. You can trust Him, even if you feel unsure whether you can trust a particular area of your husband's life.

And also remember that this hasn't changed *anything* about your husband—he is still the same person he was before you started learning all this stuff. If he's a God-honoring man who works diligently to maintain a thought life of integrity, then he's still that man! And if he has some real issues to address, now you hopefully understand him much better, and can prayerfully figure out what you can and should do. This knowledge doesn't need to change your relationship for anything other than the better.

Perhaps you still don't even know where your husband or boyfriend is on all of this, and your head is spinning with possibilities and worries about what might really be going on. If so, that's okay. Just don't let it spin so rapidly that you get overwhelmed, and don't let those possibilities subtly morph into you thinking that they're realities. Until you talk with your man, you won't know what any of his realities are.

And if you're wondering about all the different ways this discussion can spin out, we have some practical advice lined up for you in the FAQ section. Finish the book before you do anything rash with (or to!) your husband.

But perhaps now you're wondering how this stuff affects your son. What should you do about it? That's what the next chapter is all about.

9

The Mom's Response

Moms, you are so crucial to your children's development, as well as to their perceptions of healthy sexuality. We'll get to being the parent of a visually wired son shortly, but first, let's talk about being a parent, period. Your kids—both sons and daughters—are paying attention to you, and they see how you treat sex and react to it in our culture. Your sons are looking to you as an example of how to interact *with* a woman, while your daughters are looking to you as an example of how to *be* a woman. And the kicker is this: they're going to learn a lot more about these things based on how you act than on what you say.

So the question becomes, what are you teaching them?

How do you act when you see sexualized advertisements on television? What about when you go to the beach or the pool? when you walk past the Victoria's Secret store at the mall? Do you ignore it? laugh? make a face? try to hustle your son past as if you're scared of it? use it as an opportunity to teach a principle or open up a conversation?

Now, a quick caveat: we know this all can be difficult to talk about, and we also know you don't need yet another reason to worry about whether you're doing enough for your kids. If you're like me (Shaunti), you're probably already too hard on yourself! We know how often you second-guess yourself—after all, both of us are parents too!

So take a deep breath and relax. You don't need to turn into some sort of how-to-talk-about-sex expert. But you do need to be intentional about handling this issue in a healthy way instead of a way that could ultimately confuse your kids or lead to problems later on. Because the reality is, you are sending them a message of one type or another no matter what.

If they see you look embarrassed and shut down when one of *those* songs comes on the radio, that sends a message. ("We can't talk about this subject.")

If you walk near the giant, provocative posters at the lingerie store and jokingly tell your teenage son, "Let's look at the Disney store across the hall, shall we?" that sends a different type of message. ("Yes, this is awkward, but I get what you're going through. And we can acknowledge the importance of looking away, but move on without a sermon.")

And by not addressing sexual issues, that sends a message too. ("I'm going to leave you to figure this out on your own.")

One of the common threads I (Craig) and the rest of my team have noticed in the work we've done with XXXchurch is that the way a parent handles and talks about sex can deeply impact a child's development, mind-set, and experiences.

When kids know they can have an open and honest discussion

with their mom or dad about sex, they are less likely to step into sexual minefields like pornography or sexual encounters with their peers. But that almost certainly means that Mom or Dad needs to initiate those open and honest discussions. Being proactive isn't an option; it is a 100 percent necessity. And that type of conversation will be helpful because it shows you're open, even if it feels awkward or as if you're fumbling a bit. You are making the effort and showing you care—and that counts for a lot.

With all this in mind, it's imperative that you open up. Talk with your kids—especially during those unexpected window-of-opportunity moments. If you see guys at the mall openly leering at some teen girls, use it as a chance to talk with your sons about how they want to look at and treat women. If you see your young son trying very hard not to stare at the bikini-clad girl on the beach, thank him for working to respect girls but also let him know how God created his mind to work, so that he can gain a better understanding about himself and his sexuality and what to do with those very normal feelings that are awakening. Now that you have a better idea of how men think visually, talk with your daughters about it so they can know how to relate to guys in healthy ways that also honor their own femininity.

> When kids know they can have an open and honest discussion with their mom or dad about sex, they are less likely to step into sexual minefields.

When you calmly talk to your kids about sexual stuff in a matter-of-fact way, your kids will talk to you about it too.

We mentioned earlier that it's best if your husband can be the one to talk with your son about his visual stimulation—at least the first time. After all, they'll understand each other much better and may not have the sort of language/translation breakdown that you might have. However, we do understand that might not be an option for every mom, so we're going to give you some basics for how you can respond to your son—both in conversation and in action. But this is just a starting point. Entire books have been written about the different issues that come along with this topic, including one by me (Craig) called *Touchy Subjects: Talking to Kids About Sex, Tech, and Social Media in a Touchscreen World*, and we suggest you dive into those for more specialized guidance.

But to get you started, below are a few simple pointers.

Don't Wait

Your kids are going to find out about stuff sooner rather than later. In fact, even if your son is very young, he is already processing the world visually. The stuff he's seeing is having an impact on him whether you want it to or not, so rather than wait around for him to start developing warped ideas that get even further warped by the culture around him, take the initiative and open the door to conversation and action. I (Craig) suggest talking to your boys about guarding their eyes and honoring God from the earliest ages, and then about sex and these topics in general terms starting between the ages of seven and nine. Then of course continue the conversation and get more specific throughout the following years.

Pick Your Spot—and Be Ready to Listen

Ah, but what's the best way to open that door? You've probably figured out that it isn't a good idea to just blurt something out at the dinner table. This is why I recommend that you look for the world to give you opportunities to talk about this stuff with your son. When you keep your eyes open for those opportunities, the world will inevitably dump them in your lap very quickly.

So keep your eyes peeled, and then when you see an opening to start a discreet conversation or suggest an important action, take it.

When you do have a conversation, it will tend to go much better when you take the position of an interviewer rather than a preacher. You know how kids are: the longer you talk, the more they tune out. So instead of holding forth at length at them, ask them an introductory question. ("What do you think of that advertisement?" "Those girls at the pool are all in bikinis; does that bother you?" "Did you notice that woman? When she wears that, what do you think she is saying about herself? What does your noticing her say about you?") Then listen to their answers.

Look, we get it—if you're talking to your sons, they're probably going to be embarrassed. And even if they're on board with having the conversation, very few adolescent males are going to turn into chatterboxes about anything, let alone this topic. So listen, take what you can get and realize that there will be more opportunities to talk later on. You don't have to cover the whole subject all at once.

One way to reach teenage boys, in fact, is to use their awakening interest and confusion about how females think to share a few carefully chosen words on your reaction as a woman to some of those images. ("Do you think the girl in that outfit is looking for attention? Yeah? You know, we women sometimes seek attention because we're insecure. Have you seen examples of that?")

Also realize that as you are talking to your son, direct eye contact can sometimes stimulate a fight-or-flight reaction in the male brain. So try to maneuver yourself into a side-by-side position if you want to talk. For example, you might wait until you are walking away from the pool to ask about whether the bikinis ever bother him, or until you are driving home to ask why he thinks that girl at the mall might have worn that particular outfit.

Don't Freak Out

We feel a bit like a broken record, but if keeping calm is important with a husband, it is essential with a son: if you want him to share things with you, you *must* stay calm, politely interested, and composed, no matter what he is sharing.

Now, that said, if he's emotional about something, be the empathetic mom. And draw out his feelings by asking him what he thinks and feels about the situation. Give him time to process, and come back and talk about stuff another day if need be. Or give him a hug, if that is what he needs. But no matter what, stay unfazed and steady. He will feel much more secure confiding in you. (If you need to, you can always freak out later, when you're talking with a girlfriend or with your husband!)

> The more calm and matter-of-fact you can be in talking about this subject, the more likely it is that your son will be open with you for years to come.

Now, it is important to realize that many of our young sons will be in the Innocently Curious category when they see a sexy commercial or a woman dressed provocatively. And even boys from godly families will experiment with self-stimulation in one form or another as they grow. (More on that in the FAQ section.) We must not make them feel like they are perverts simply because they are curious. If we do, that will completely shut the door to our ability to influence them in a good direction. Many boys—especially preteens and teens—will be wary of having this type of conversation anyway. The more calm and matter-of-fact you can be in talking about this subject—especially if there are some real issues to work through!—the more likely it is that your son will be open with you for years to come.

Just as important, the more calm you are, the more you demonstrate that sexual desires themselves aren't bad—that this is how we are made, but that God wants those desires to be fully expressed only in marriage.

Teach Honorable Behavior

This is best coming from (and modeled by) a dad to a son, but we know that isn't always possible in every circumstance. But in general, there are a few tips that a dad (or you) can teach a son from the earliest age:

- *"Be careful little eyes what you see."* Because I (Shaunti) had been researching men and this subject even before my son was born, my husband and I used the children's song to start talking with our kids when they were very young about the need to care about what we let into our minds. Even something simple like "That is a scary television show. Maybe we shouldn't let that into our eyes," gave us a way to say later "That seems like an inappropriate television show. Maybe we shouldn't watch that again."

- *"Eyes down."* Many families use this type of technique. We have some friends who, ever since their sons were young, have gently or jokingly said "eyes down" whenever a potentially inappropriate commercial or scene comes on when they are watching television as a family. And today, when their boys are tall, strapping teenagers who look and sound like men, they still look down when needed, even though no one says "eyes down" anymore. Everyone in the family lowers their eyes for a few moments, then the mom glances up, checking to see when it's safe for everyone to continue watching. They don't make a big deal out of it, and they make sure their boys know that this is just stuff they are going to face in this culture. But by developing this habit, they also show that, as a family, they are trying to honor God and keep their thought lives pure.

- *"Bounce your eyes."* Similarly, many dads teach their sons the habit of bouncing their eyes away whenever they land on a voluptuous or sensuous sight that they would otherwise really want to look at. These boys are taught the habit of looking away quickly so that the temptation doesn't take hold—and many men continue this habit for the rest of their lives.

- *"Redirect your thoughts."* Just like we teach our kids to redirect their grumbling thoughts to a good attitude about an annoying task (homework, yard chores, taking out the trash), we can teach our older boys to redirect their sensuous thoughts to math problems, cars, or even Scripture when a visual image or sensual thought enters their brains that would not honor that girl, and would not honor God. It is also important to give them a vision for the future, by saying something like, "When you're married, you'll be able to redirect your thoughts to your wife."

- *"Are you being accountable/safe about media?"* Very important: don't allow your kids to be on the Internet in a private room or online without a filter. You run too great of a risk when you put a computer with Internet access in their bedroom or allow them to take an unmonitored iPad wherever they go. There are so many great options to help you as a parent learn more about where your kids are going online, the apps they are interacting with, and websites that they are visiting. This is a specialized area, so look at some specialized resources such as Craig's books. Check out X3watch.com for Internet-filtering solutions (including on smartphones and other mobile devices), and visit our website for parents called iParent.tv to learn more about what your kids are really doing online. We have linked to all of these and included some special offers on other resources at MenAreVisual.com/resources.

Be Honest

Kids today seem to be more savvy about truth and honesty than any of us ever were when we were kids. They have very finely tuned lie detectors and can tell when you're not being forthright with them, so don't even try. You don't have to be viscerally blunt, but don't sugarcoat things for them either. Speak appropriately to their age level and give them credit for being smarter than you might think. If they ask you about your own adolescence, be honest. If they ask you about what's going on in the world, be honest. If they ask blunt questions about sexuality, be honest.

Have Grace for Them—and for Yourself

In the midst of that honesty, be sure to saturate it with grace—not just for them but also for yourself. Again, we understand that you're doing the best you can, so go easy on yourself and on them. It's a heavy enough topic; there's no need to add a load of guilt to the discussion as well.

Keep the Conversation Going for the Long Run

Parenting is a long-term proposition, which is actually one of the great things about it. Can you imagine how difficult it would be if you only had one short sprint when it came to parenting your kids? How much pressure would that create? What if you got something wrong?

Fortunately, that's not what we have going on; instead, we have a long road of parenting that has many twists and turns along the way. We get to nudge our kids down that road and continue to influence their lives for years. So keep talking with them about sex, perception, visual temptations, and anything else they need to know to equip them to live healthy, happy, godly lives.

And if you prove a safe listener, you may be surprised at how much even your not-very-talkative sons *do* tell you from time to time.

Not long ago, I (Shaunti) asked a new acquaintance to read an early draft of this book. She has a husband and two teen boys, ages sixteen and thirteen. In other words, her house was a petri dish for the stuff we've been talking about! She shared a really interesting example of how her efforts to be a listening ear had paid off:

> Even before I had Danny, my oldest, I was already worried about how was I going to parent a middle school or high school boy in today's culture. This is one reason I was so

grateful for a husband who would be a great father, but still. So their whole lives, I thought, *Okay, I need to learn to listen to them.* So I would ask questions, and listen. And I realized the more I looked calm and unfazed by things, the more they would tell me.

My husband has tried to teach them how to redirect their eyes. Like, he would see the voluptuous girl about to walk by in her spaghetti-strap top and say something like "Whoops, there's a Nike," which means "Yikes, temptation coming; look at your Nike sneakers." That was our little code, even though they don't really need it anymore.

So when I was in the middle of reading the draft of your book, I realized . . . we hadn't talked about it in a while. And the day before, we had been at a girls' high school volleyball game and you know what those girls wear. So I decided to ask Danny about it when we were in the car, side by side, so it would be less threatening.

I said, "I've been reading about this, and I don't really understand how this works because I'm a girl. Just like you don't understand why I cry all the time, I don't understand how guys are visual. You know how we've talked about Nike, about looking away. But still, do you ever struggle with this?"

He said, "I really don't have a problem with it, because you and Dad have told me my whole life to bounce my eyes."

And I said, "Thank you for telling me that. But it doesn't mean it will always be easy, so please talk to us if you need to."

Then I started to think to myself, *How does he handle the fact that teen boys are apparently always getting an erection when they see certain sights?*

So believe it or not, I asked him. I said, "Okay, this is an awkward thing, but I know a guy's body reacts physically when you see things like those girls in spandex shorts at the volleyball game. And you were wearing sweatpants yesterday. Is that ever a problem for you?"

Without blinking an eye, he told me, "Nah, I was wearing compression shorts. So it was okay."

Part of me couldn't believe he told me that. But I was so glad that he felt able to talk about it with me! That was really encouraging.

As I listened to her, I thought, *That is really encouraging!* As a mom of a preteen boy myself, it is encouraging to think that maybe, just maybe, if I can be a safe listener, he'll be that open with me someday.

Moral of the story: don't just assume that your kids are okay. Take the initiative. Open up conversations with them in sensitive, discreet, and humorous ways. That last point is especially important—you'd be surprised at how far a sense of humor can go in lightening a conversation and creating some spontaneous insight and parent/child bonding. Sex is no joke, obviously, but talking about it can be more fun if you add humor to the mix.

> You'd be surprised at how far a sense of humor can go in lightening a conversation.

Do it for your kids. They may kick and scream and plug their ears, but they'll thank you for it eventually.

10

Living
in Hope

A s you process everything you've learned so far about the minds of men, your own mind may be buzzing. You may be thrilled to finally know more about your man or your son, or you may be thinking that moving to a planet populated only by women sounds pretty appealing right now. You may feel able to implement the various suggestions, or you may feel a lot like that ostrich who is looking for a nice patch of sand in which to hide her head.

Some of you may be wondering, *Has it even been worth it to take this journey?* Or, *Should I bother to continue it once I turn the last page of this book?*

Yes. We firmly believe it's worth it. Even if the journey is hard, it's worth it.

As we said at the outset, your husband is the same person he was before you started reading this book. Your son is the same boy. The only difference is that now you know him better. You are trying to understand something that God has built into him, that causes a tug of war inside him, but which is intended for *good*. You are, we hope, now motivated to walk this road *with* him. A road that he's been walking all along.

In other words, he's no longer alone, and neither are you. This is a journey you're now taking together. So if you can walk through any rough patches with God-given love, grace, compassion, humor, kindness, wisdom, perseverance, and strength, you'll end up with a level of closeness that you may never have had before.

Not long ago on a FamilyLife Today radio broadcast, pastor Ted Cunningham shared from his excellent book *Fun Loving You* about the importance of not taking marriage so seriously all the time and being willing to enjoy each other and have fun as best friends.

When the radio hosts, Dennis Rainey and Bob Lepine, asked Ted how he and his wife got to the point of being able to do that, we were struck by his explanation. He said that things changed once he and his wife, Amy, had walked through a difficult season that involved openly discussing things they didn't usually talk about—and sometimes didn't want to talk about! With nothing hidden, and with each one trying to understand the other, they were led into an entirely new level of oneness and true friendship—and an entirely new level of marriage that they never before knew existed.

> Your husband is the same person he was before you started reading this book. Your son is the same boy. The only difference is that now you know him better.

We were even more struck that what precipitated this rather difficult soul-searching season was a discussion about the very issues we've been tackling in this book. We want to share Ted's story[26] in his own words, as an example to you of the power of being willing to go on this journey. Although this is a fairly long excerpt, it demonstrates the power of being transparent and able to discuss these topics—and the hope that rises up as a result.

TED: [In marriage, people] want to enjoy life together. I tell the young guys in our church . . . who are finding their romance in porn and their adventure in video games: "Listen, guys, you don't have to choose between life and a wife. You can have both at the exact same time. Don't go with the culture that says, "Marriage is going to be miserable." . . . You can decide the quality you are going to bring into marriage. . . .

DENNIS: So, you have been married since 1996. Ever had a dark moment in those years?

TED: Yes, I would say the first seven years, like most couples, were the toughest. Those were the "I'm going to blame you for all of my unhappiness." . . . Most young couples are in this same boat: plugged into one another as the source of life, dependent on one another for happiness. . . .

I remember [when things first changed. Amy] was in bed, reading a book on how men think. . . . It was Shaunti Feldhahn's book, *For Women Only*. . . . And she is turning the pages, and I just remember her getting mad—I mean, frustrated. She puts the book down, and she says, "I've got to ask you a question." And I'm like, {dramatic sigh} *This is not going to be good.* We'd been married just seven years. And she goes, "I want to know: have you ever struggled with lust toward another woman?"

Now, let me teach all the listeners something. . . . You start acting as though you didn't hear the question. I said, "Huh?!" And she said, "Have you ever struggled with lust toward another woman?" So you go to tactic two: you act as if you didn't understand the question. "What do you mean?" And then, I knew we were going there.

See, there are three parts of a man's heart. There is that public part we'll share with that stranger on the street. There is the private part we'll share with family and friends. But then, there's that third part that we don't want to let anyone into. That part we don't want anyone to know about—we try to hide from God Himself. And I just knew that we were going to have this *long* conversation about the way men think. And how her—at that time—twenty-nine-year-old husband, [a seminary graduate], was still keeping the secret of how men think.

So, Shaunti and I are friends now, but we weren't for years. . . .

DENNIS: Why do men avoid opening up their hearts to their wives? . . .

TED: Safety. They don't feel safe. I have to be in a judgment-free zone before I'll share. I've been to men's events [at which] guys who are speakers say things like, "Let's just admit it, guys, there are a lot of things we can't share with our wives." I always cringe and kind of bristle when I hear that. Do we really want that message out there? That there should be things that I share at a seven o'clock men's prayer breakfast that I can't share with my wife?"

I would rather give the message, "Let's create safety in the home. Let's create an environment where I can share openly, and my wife can share openly with me." [Because] I remember that week [after my wife asked me that]—it was like mourning a death for a week. It was not good.

DENNIS: So, the truth came out.

TED: Yes.

DENNIS: That you struggled?

TED: That [men] struggle, yes. And I remember first sharing this with her, going, "How did you not know this? We went to [a major Christian university]!" We heard countless talks on this. But now, it's in her marriage. Now, it's her marriage and she's going, "I want to just figure this out."

Boy, you want to talk about a week with difficult, painful conversations. I even watched her when we would go into stores, looking—

> "Let's create safety in the home. Let's create an environment where I can share openly, and my wife can share openly with me."

BOB: Looking where you were looking?

TED: Where I was looking, and where every man in the place was looking . . . like, "Where are the eyes in this room right now?"

DENNIS: I want you to speak to a wife who is thinking about asking the question right now. . . . What do you want her to know before she asks that question?

TED: Before you ask him this question, ask yourself: *Am I safe? Can I, right now, be trusted with the answer that I know I'm going to get?*

BOB: Yes. *If he says "I struggle," how am I going to respond to this?*

DENNIS: I would agree with you, because I shared a story of how, early in our marriage, I confessed to my wife I was struggling with lust . . . I've shared that story publicly, and I've had men come up to me after the message and say, "I

could *never* share that with my wife. She would fall apart.
She would think she is not enough for me—I'm not
satisfied with her." That's the way a lot of women think.

TED: Yes. . . . But that conversation seven years into our
marriage, it was the *best* thing that ever happened to our
marriage. . . . In our case, even within a couple of weeks,
Amy said, "I, Ted Cunningham, want to be your only
fantasy. Not number one; your *only* fantasy. I want to be
the one you're thinking of." . . . There is a Hebrew term for
that, and the Hebrew term is *bam-bam-chicka-bam-bam*
{catcall noises}. . . . That's from Dallas Theological
Seminary.

DENNIS: I was reviewing my Hebrew, and I don't remember
that term. . . .

{laughter}

TED: And I would say the *Fun Loving You* message is that you
have to have the hard conversation to get to the fun in
almost every single area. . . . We want to find every
frustrating aspect of marriage and find a way to decide how
to enjoy that. We're done changing each other. We're done
fixing each other. We're done blaming each other. We don't
want to be plugged into one another as a source of life. We
want to plug into the true and only source of life, Jesus.
And the best marriages on the planet are where husband
and wife are both plugged into the true and only source of
life and giving one another the overflow. That's the type of
marriage we want. . . . And it is difficult, it is painful, but
what we need young people to see—what I shared with
you—is the joy that comes out of that.

Yes, this can be a difficult thing to address. It can be awkward. But from that awkwardness comes awareness. Sensitivity becomes security. Transparency leads to trust. Difficulty turns to delight.

We know that not everyone is at that point. We know many hard situations can arise along the way (and we address many in the FAQ section that follows). Hurtful actions, painful memories, selfishness, or the consequences of poor choices can appear as giant cracks in the road; cracks that can seem like impossible-to-cross chasms.

Wherever you are, we would simply encourage you with this: when you see those chasms, ask God to show you your next steps. Cling to Him. Trust Him whether or not you can trust the man in your life. And just as in Ted Cunningham's story, you might find that He is taking you across a bridge to a more beautiful place than you could have imagined.

> It is worth it to press forward in understanding.

It is worth it to press forward in understanding. And two people who are, finally, together in awareness, mutual security, and trust will find that the journey is worth it.

Frequently Asked Questions

I (Craig) have found that one of the great things about running a ministry like XXXchurch is being able to respond to all kinds of questions that people—especially women—have about pornography, this sexualized culture, and the effects it can have on society, their marriages, their spouses, and their kids.

We encourage these questions. After all, that's how we learn: by asking questions. So at XXXchurch.com we've established as a fundamental principle that there is no such thing as a wrong question. Our visitors, whether they're regular readers or new to the site, are encouraged to submit questions related to anything they might be wondering about.

As you can imagine, some of the questions we get are from people who have nowhere else to turn or who are embarking into the frightful, worried world of loving someone who is hooked on porn. Sometimes those visitors are angry, sometimes they're afraid, sometimes they're depressed, sometimes they're hopeless . . . and more often than not, they're some combination of all those. Often they're not certain what they're feeling at any given moment, or how to describe it. Conflicting emotions can be felt at the same time, and many of the visitors to XXXchurch.com reflect that truth.

Their questions also reflect their uncertainty. And so what we try to do is answer them as honestly, delicately, and discreetly as we can, while still being realistic about the situation they might be in. And we are encouraging about the kinds of relational healing available. Because there is often so much more hope than they are seeing right now.

In this chapter, we'll tackle a few of our most frequently asked questions, and suggest some answers. Some are pretty basic answers, because the true solution to some of these is "You need specialized help." We understand that not every question will apply to your specific situation, but we hope you'll find some answers either for yourself or for someone else you are helping along the way.

We also urge you not to review this FAQ section until you have read through the rest of the book. That knowledge will help keep you from potentially misinterpreting our guidance in the pages ahead.

It bothers me that my son might be masturbating— especially since he's presumably fantasizing while he does. Isn't that lust and adultery according to Jesus? What do I do?

Nothing like starting off the FAQ section with a bang!

First of all, let's acknowledge that there is never going to be one right, obvious solution to this. It simply isn't covered in the Bible, and respected experts are all over the map on whether it is a big deal or not.

Second, though, let's put this topic in perspective. Most moms tend to flip out about this, while most dads don't. Why? Because all men were young men once, and so they recognize that self-stimulation is something that most teenage boys deal with to one degree or another. Which, honestly, is not surprising in a culture that constantly stimulates them visually, even if they are trying to do everything right. So there is a great need for compassion. (And if your son is younger, realize there is a big difference in a young boy discovering his body and masturbating as opposed to a teenager for whom this has become a chronic compulsion, especially if porn is involved.)

Since every boy and every situation is different, we're not sure there is any one perfect answer to how to guide a boy in this area other than to do the best you can do to encourage him to honor God in every area of his life, including his sexuality. If porn is involved, take the steps we've talked about in this book, including getting him help if necessary, then trust God with the outcome. No matter what, God will be working in your son's life.

And remember that you cannot control what happens in your son's brain. Only he can. You can worry all you want, but worrying will not put pure thoughts into your son's mind. That's all up to him.

So what can you do? Most important, you can pray for him. That's a must—and it's something you're probably already doing! It also isn't just a platitude. This whole issue is essentially about a battle for the hearts and minds of our kids, so it is primarily a *spiritual* battle. We need all the other action steps discussed in this book, but without prayer we would be neglecting the most important step. I (Shaunti) can't tell you the number of men I have spoken with who have told me that they feel absolutely certain the reason they have never badly struggled with porn—despite some poor choices along the way!—is that their mothers were praying for them for years. The fervent prayer of a mother is powerful and effective.

In addition, keep the lines of calm communication open between your son and you (and your spouse), and do your best to limit any negative influences that might crop up. When you encounter things that might get him stirred up visually, whether in the media or the real world, you can turn it into a lesson about the hypersexualization of our culture or the objectification of women or even how God has created us to feel desire. Just take the lead and talk about it with him—as long as you can do so in the calm way discussed in chapter 9.

As for the part about adultery according to Jesus, I (Craig) tend to read the Sermon on the Mount not so much as a list of prescribed actions or rules not to break and more as a lengthy lesson in the fact that Jesus primarily wants your *heart*. If you're a person of faith, teach your son to point his heart in God's direction, knowing that if he does, it is far more likely that he will end up with the positive behaviors you are hoping for.

My husband and I are in our twenties, and we have been dealing with the digital age all our lives. Won't my husband have been somewhat desensitized to this stuff? Does it really impact him in the same way as someone older?

Somewhat desensitized? Possibly. Completely desensitized? Impossible. Yes, the fact that you and your husband are in your twenties means you have probably both been exposed to more things in a shorter amount of time than someone like me (Craig) who is approaching forty. Your generation has seen too much too soon, and while your husband might be desensitized to some of this stuff, that doesn't mean it hasn't shaped him or affected him. He can't change the fact that he has a male brain.

I have a suspicion that, while this stuff sneaks up and hits the older generation a bit more, younger people in their twenties who have been bombarded almost daily are not immune. You still must be willing to talk through this issue with him and not just assume he is unaffected by it. He may be affected differently than an older person, but I have a hard time believing he hasn't been affected at all.

My husband sometimes looks at women walking by. What do I do?

You have to determine whether the sideways glance is just a knee-jerk reaction on his part, or whether he's actually *looking*. After all, think about this: don't *you* notice those women too? That's not unusual for anyone. Expecting your husband to not ever notice or glance at an attractive woman would be like expecting you to not ever notice or glance either. That's not reality. After all, does he notice a beautiful sunset or an eye-catching car? There's nothing wrong with noticing beauty. And it is almost impossible to not be startled by something startling!

The problems come when there is intentionality behind his looking. For example, more of a lingering glance because he is spinning up some impure thoughts. And if so, it can be incredibly demeaning and frustrating to see your husband's eyes wander toward the body of some attractive woman as she walks past in the restaurant, on the train, in the grocery store, or even at church!

Like we discussed, a man cannot avoid noticing the woman who is dressed to call overt attention to her body, but he can choose not to look or continue looking. So first, remember that for a man not to look, it takes an intentional effort to counterprogram the biological urge we covered in chapter 2. And even if he is successful, at times, a man will likely be very aware that the woman is there and he'll be fighting the desire to look the whole time.

Second, if he does sometimes look at the woman walking by, remember for most men, this is less like a lust-filled predatory behavior (like looking for a sexual partner) and instead is more like a bad habit (like chewing with his mouth open or leaving the toilet seat up).

Third, if your husband is generally an all-around good guy and faithful husband who nevertheless occasionally takes a lingering look at another woman, you first need to let him know how you feel about it. As noted, some women really don't have a problem with it because they know it doesn't say anything about *them*. Other women realize their husband truly is just appreciating beauty and is not mentally undressing the pretty twenty-something who just walked by. But if you are bothered by that type of look and suspect there are some inappropriate thoughts going on, ask him to respectfully consider breaking that habit. Go through the action steps we suggested in earlier chapters as you start your conversation.

Once the two of you are on the same page, if you recognize the situation is not serious enough to need other intervention, and your man is fully willing to break his bad habit, you can try to set up some sort of system between you. Something to motivate him to alter his behavior, perhaps even using humor to defuse situations where his roving eye returns. Now, this won't work if he really doesn't want you trying to catch him. But if the two of you have the type of relationship in which he welcomes the habit-breaking help, come up with a process that both of you are okay with. Maybe any time you catch him looking, you have permission to teasingly punch him in the arm, or use a particular catch phrase. Or if humor seems inappropriate in your situation, work out a phrase that is more respectful. ("Honey, could you come over this way?") There isn't one technique that works; what works is agreeing to something ahead of time and then rolling with it.

No matter what, trust that your man loves you and has the best of intentions for honoring your feelings. Yes, he's not going to be perfect, but he's going to try to get there.

But what if he's unwilling to stop and is defiant about looking, regularly, even though it bothers you? If that's the case, then he has a bigger problem; there's a heart issue that he needs to address, and he may not yet be willing to. So even if he won't seek help, we strongly suggest that you yourself seek counsel and advice from a qualified marriage counselor.

I suspect my husband is looking at porn, but I'm not sure. What do I do?

There is so much subtlety and sensitivity wrapped up in this question. On its surface, it seems pretty easy to answer, but this tends to be one of those instances where the question itself hides a few layers of doubt, fear, and worry. How so? Let's look at three reasons women ask this question: trust, anger, and fear.

Some women ask this question because they don't want to break trust or be perceived as snooping by their husbands. You love your husband—or at least you did at one point. You loved him enough to marry him. But so much of love—especially when it comes to the love between husband and wife—is the ability to trust one another. When you said your vows, you pledged yourselves to each other, forsaking all other marital-type relationships. You and your husband made a promise to each other that the two of you would be all that you'd need in your marriage.

The mere fact that you're asking this question means there might be a third party: the mistress, porn. And that can be devastating for a variety of reasons, but one of those reasons is the persistent, gnawing suspicion that you might be right, followed by the equally persistent, gnawing reply: *But what if I'm wrong?*

So let's consider the options. If your instincts are correct and your husband is indeed looking at porn, then you owe it to him, yourself, and your marriage to start dealing with it as quickly as possible. The porn problem won't go away on its own.

And if you're wrong? Then good! You can breathe easily knowing that you won't have to deal with watching your husband wrestle against the insidious tentacles of pornography.

But you need to discuss it and find out. For a marriage to work, you and your husband have to honor each other's feelings as genuine; after all, you likely wouldn't be suspicious unless you had a real reason to think that something was going on, in which case it is important for you to check it out. Hopefully once you ask about it (see below for more on how to do that) he will understand that. And if your suspicions prove unfounded, then the two of you can work together on determining why you felt porn might be a problem and what both you and he can do to alleviate those feelings—which will bring you closer together.

Now, I (Craig) would caution you on one thing. We said "honor each other's feelings as genuine," but there is a very important exception: when you suspect he might be lying to you. Women, at least my wife, have this great thing called women's intuition. You could be spot on with your suspicions and even have full-blown proof, but many men will lie, even when confronted with the facts. Their reason for doing so is not unlike that of a typical child. It's sort of like how my then-nine-year-old daughter reacted after lying to us about something three times in a row. When I asked her why she lied, she said, "Because I knew I would get in trouble."

I then said, "Elise, what happens when you lie?"

She said, "I get in more trouble."

So, why did she lie? She knew she would get in even bigger

trouble if we caught her lying, but because of her overwhelming guilt and shame, she was willing to take that chance. And she was also willing to gamble to see if she could get away with it. Adults aren't unlike kids in this regard. If this is the case with your man, don't push him yet. The more he knows that you know, and the more you are aware of this, the sooner and easier this will come to the surface. I would encourage you to pray that if there is an issue (and be willing to believe there may not be!), God brings it out into the open, where it is easier to deal with. When it is in hiding, it is extremely difficult to process through.

Some women ask this question out of anger at their husbands for something else happening in their marriage, and they are hoping to catch their husbands in order to prove a point. If this is you, I (Craig) feel for you. I honestly do. I'm guessing that you didn't get married in order to be in a constant state of anger and frustration, fighting with your husband all the time, and feeling you and/or your marriage get devalued at every turn. Whether or not these feelings are justified, they are honest and true for you right now, and you are angry.

But then our question for you would be: When has acting out of blind rage ever been a good thing? This isn't any small thing we're talking about here—this is your marriage! This is a lifelong commitment of love you've made to another person, so regardless of how you feel about your husband right now, you owe it to him to respond to whatever instincts you might be having with as much consideration as possible. The "Gotcha!" game rarely works out well for the person doing the "Gotcha." After all, if your husband is an awful, no-good person, that truth will come out eventually. But if he's not and you act as if he is, you're going to do some damage to your relationship that may take a while to repair.

So instead of trying to set a trap for your husband, we recommend that you take a moment or two (or ten or ten thousand) to cool down. Maybe bounce your feelings off of a trusted friend or counselor. Just make sure—and this is vitally important!—that it is someone with a level head and a godly focus, and someone who you can trust to help you fight for your marriage, not just your "rights." Then move forward with the action steps we'll detail below.

And finally, *some women ask this question because they're afraid they already know the answer, but are trying to convince themselves otherwise.* Perhaps you can relate. You suspect this might be true about your husband, but you desperately hope it isn't. Maybe you even know deep down that your husband has a porn problem but you're trying to convince yourself that he doesn't, that you're seeing things, that you're attributing behavior to him that doesn't really line up with his character.

Again, the porn problem—if it is real for your husband—isn't going to go away on its own. This is not something that gets better when ignored. It's also possible that his problem will only worsen, making him more emboldened the longer he gets away with his secret.

Reality is always better than worry, so we recommend that you deal with whatever feelings you have and unearth the truth of whatever is causing you to ask this question to begin with.

What to do. Now that we've established three of the possible reasons you might be asking this question, let's put the rubber to the road and talk about what you should actually do in this type of situation.

It's hard, because this can be a topic that is filled with emotional turmoil. You may feel fearful, cheated, abused, dejected, rejected, hopeless, numb, angry, or any combination of those—or you may feel none of those things. *These feelings are okay.* But right now, you can't give in to those feelings, because the fact of the matter is that you don't know the truth.

Yet.

And that's what you're trying to discover.

There's likely a reason that you are even wondering about his possible interaction with pornography. Perhaps he has been very moody or is spending too much free time alone with his computer or mobile device. Maybe there are unexplained charges on the credit card. Maybe he's said something or done something in the bedroom to raise your suspicions.

Whatever the reason, you have something in your mind, your soul, or your gut that is telling you that porn might be a problem. So we would encourage you to honor that in yourself and follow up on it. Take some time away from the kids, away from the distractions of life, and sit down with your husband, and plainly and honestly express your concerns to him.

We've mentioned this before regarding other conversations you might want to have with your husband about his visual nature, but it's worth repeating: don't treat this initial conversation as anything other than an invitation to explore the subject openly and honestly. Show your man that you can handle whatever he has to share—as long as it's the truth. Then, as a second step, you can consider it a fact-finding mission; think almost like a respectful journalist working to understand a story. Maybe there's going to be a big story here, or maybe your fears will be unfounded and you will learn that he's only wrestling in a minor way. Either way, the best way to get the facts is to be safe to talk to, as well as determined, compassionate, and rational.

If you don't have serious concerns but are just wondering, here's an example of how a woman could bring it up in a way that would likely increase the chance of an honest reply without defensiveness:

First, find something porn-related in the news—you won't have to look hard; there's almost always something in the news about pornography or sexual addiction. Then use that as a means of bringing up the topic to your husband. This is a way to introduce the topic of porn in a timely, conversational way rather than just coming out with a blunt, scary-to-him question like "What's up with you and porn?"

You might say something like, "I was looking at the news today and saw [fill in the blank]. What do you think about that?" Once you have his answer, you can navigate the conversation toward the question. Perhaps you can say something like, "I was reading up on this and found out that many men were exposed to pornography when they were kids. Was that true for you?" Or, "Is it true that all guys have seen porn?" Just try to frame the question as naturally and inquisitively as possible, asking not *only about your husband* but also *about men in general.* This will help him to understand that you aren't leveling the cannons at him specifically; you're just trying to find out what's up.

Sex therapist Dr. Michael Sytsma added this advice: "Do this calmly, and take it slowly. Only move forward if the cement seems to have set enough to hold the weight of the subject. Otherwise, keep laying the foundation and letting it cure as you slowly move further. It may need to be in a future conversation that you come back to it and begin to ask the more personal questions about what he is doing now."

I know that trying to pin down the truth about this can be difficult. It might even feel impossible. But if you have reason for concern, you need to try, and above all you need to remember what we have kept emphasizing in this book: *Your husband can have a porn problem and still love you more than his own life.* And if he does have a problem, remember that this is not your fault. And it doesn't mean he doesn't love you or find you attractive.

Remember all the principles you've learned in this book, then pray and believe that the Holy Spirit will be leading you as you embark on the conversation.

My husband has been regularly looking at porn, and I caught him. What do I do?

First off: we're so sorry. That is a horrible way to find out about the secret your husband has been keeping from you, and if you feel betrayed right now, that is very real and very okay. Or maybe you don't feel betrayed—just hurt and disappointed for you and sad for him. It is normal to have any of those feelings.

So, what can you do? Or more importantly, what *should* you do? There are many different possibilities here, and as we have said, whole ministries dedicated to walking a husband and wife through this exact season in the right way for their specific situation. We would urge you to seek out those resources (some are listed at MenAreVisual.com/resources, including support small groups for spouses) and get the specific help you need. But we can also offer some general help as well.

The first thing we want you to do is to internalize this truth: *you are not alone.* Many other women have been where you are right now. Still others have yet to be where you are right now, but one day will be.

So even though it might feel like you're in this alone, we hope you can find some small comfort in knowing that there are plenty of other women who have endured this trial and have come out on the other side with stronger identities, stronger love, and a stronger marriage.

Really. A stronger marriage. It *is* possible.

The second thing we want you to realize is that your husband's porn usage is *his problem,* not yours. It's tied up with a lot of things, especially with his visual nature, but you may find it very easy to beat yourself up with a series of what-ifs:

- *What if I'd been more sexually available?*
- *What if I'd worked out more?*
- *What if I'd eaten less?*
- *What if I hadn't had a headache the other night?*
- *What if, what if, what if . . .*

Those things often *feel* like they caused your husband's porn usage, but the *fact* is, they did not.

No matter what you might want to look at in your own life and choices, *your man is the one who made the decision to look at porn.* In some cases, he may have even convinced himself that you did or said something that drove him to it—but that's just him lying to himself to avoid taking responsibility for his choices.

His use is *his issue,* not yours.

Now, that said, by deciding to use porn, your husband has brought the issue into his life. And since the two of you are one in marriage, it is now in your life as well and could have a negative effect on you and your relationship with him. So in a way, he has made it your issue.

The third thing to do is try to absorb what you have learned in this book and to think about how it applies to your man so you can eventually figure out what needs to be done about it. Try to understand *him.* What is behind his porn use?

The reason will also help you understand what was behind whatever communication he had (or didn't have) with you about it. Was your husband hiding his porn consumption, or was he open about it? If he was open in any way, the door hopefully will be open for the two of you to take the all-important step of talking things through as you make your feelings and expectations clear but show your support. Remember that because of his failure in his actions, he may feel like a complete failure as a man and most likely feels immense shame and guilt for hurting you. So here's an example of a way to start the conversation that won't let him off the hook but will still allow you to be approachable: "Honey, I love you more than anything, and I am trying to learn more about what you go through on a daily basis being a man. I know your struggle with pornography is real. I am not okay with it, but I love you and appreciate you no matter what. I want and need to talk through this with you to understand what we can do and what I can do to support you. I don't want to fight or be angry with you, but I do want to talk when you are ready."

What if he was hiding it? Then he was probably trying both to protect himself and, in a warped way, protect you from it. He knew it would likely devastate you if you found out what was going on, so he kept it a secret. That doesn't excuse it, but it might help you understand what was possibly going on in his head.

If your husband wasn't hiding his porn usage—but you also didn't really know about it or were trying to ignore it—then your relationship also has suffered from a lack of communication about this area of his life. Now you need to discover *why* you ignored it, or why he hadn't mentioned it yet. For example, did he honestly think it wouldn't bother you and so he had no need to mention it? Is he acting like you shouldn't be bothered by it or trying to make you feel unimportant or devalued for thinking that it is an issue? If that's the case, then you need to get on the same page with each other about respecting one another's opinions and feelings.

We know that navigating that can be tricky, which is why our fourth suggestion is to seek out help—but ask him to take the lead in officially getting the help. If it is a recent and/or minor problem, it may be that your husband will find the help he needs in a men's group dedicated to this issue. But many of you will need and/or want more specialized resources or counseling.

Shaunti and I have compiled a list of the best resources we have come across in our combined thirty-plus years of experience with these kinds of issues. We recommend you point your husband to this website: MenAreVisual.com/resources, then ask *him* to take the lead. Let him know that you expect him to do something about this so he is not in the same place a month or a year from now. Tell him you expect him to share what his plan is going to be to attack this area of his life once he has it figured out. When he does share his plan, feel free to suggest a few more things, if you think they are needed.

Not long ago, I worked with a couple after the wife caught her husband viewing pornography on the computer. She called me, and a few days later I went to their house. I was impressed that the husband was willing to talk to me. It wasn't going to work if it was just me talking to his wife about his problem. As we were talking, I happened to see the new smartphone on his desk, so I asked if he would consider a downgrade on that phone. He said, "You mean an upgrade?" I said, "Nope." After some discussion, we ended up at the cell phone shop and traded it in for a flip phone with no Internet capability. This didn't solve all their problems overnight, but it was a start. It was a small but important message he sent to his wife that he was willing to make real changes—a fairly big change in terms of convenience—that would protect him and help her regain trust.

Support your husband through this, but make it clear that you expect him to do the work that he needs to do.

How do I get my husband to go for counseling for his porn problem?

As some of you already know, this is a tough one. You two might need regular counseling, an intensive weekend intervention, and/or other options for help, even in addition to important steps such as his participation in a men's small group. But as you seek out those resources, make sure you let him know that you are committed to seeing it through with him, and that you want to understand and support him every step of the way. Your commitment to him and your expectation that he take the lead in this is key to moving in that direction.

In other words: you can't make him go to counseling. I (Craig) have seen this a lot at XXXchurch, where a husband goes to counseling or tries to address the problem just to make his wife happy or to, in his mind, get her off his back. But the problem with that line of motivation is that it is based entirely on another person. If something goes wrong in your relationship, whether that's a temporary fight or something worse, then he has no real motivation to continue working toward recovery. And even worse, a wife can become a convenient scapegoat: "Everything was fine until *you* made me do this counseling stuff!"

But if your husband goes to counseling or gets in a small group because he wants to better *himself*, then he has a real shot at lasting change.

So you can make all the suggestions you want, but be sure your husband knows that any solo counseling or accountability groups or anything else he does to point himself toward healthy sexuality must be done of his own volition. He needs to be the one choosing to do it, then the responsibility for maintaining it is his and his alone. But that said, having a wife who will do whatever she can to support him in the process is invaluable.

This leads to a second potential way to proceed. As therapist Dr. Michael Sytsma told us, "Him going to counseling just for him isn't the only option. She can invite him to go for counseling for *them*. Sometimes it is important to allow him to have issues with her that she is willing to work on also. Make it a team effort rather than a journey to fix *him*. If they find a skilled counselor, the counselor can help keep it balanced and moving forward."

My husband is regularly looking at porn, but he doesn't know I know. What do I do? Confront him or catch him?

We'll answer your actual question in a moment, but first, here's a big picture perspective. Since your husband doesn't know you know, then I (Craig) know one thing for sure about him: he's trying to hide his porn usage and is not doing a very good job of it, even though he thinks he is. And while that can look like hubris to the outside eye, the more likely thing is that subconsciously he knows he's letting you down, letting your marriage down, and letting himself down, and it's highly likely that he feels terrible about all that. He wants to deal with it but doesn't know how.

More than likely, your husband is not using porn out of the blue and on a whim. In fact, I'm willing to wager that he feels compelled to look at porn, and that he *feels terrible about that compulsion.*

Does that make it okay or excuse his behavior? Absolutely not. Your husband is using a visual stimulus to express himself sexually while taking intentional steps to keep you out of it. If you are like many women, finding that out can be devastating to your sense of self-esteem and self-worth. We get that.

In fact, you're probably going through a whole whirlwind of

emotions and thoughts right now, a jumble of feelings that is likely so animated that you don't feel any one certain way for a substantial length of time. That's okay and normal.

But the worst thing you can do right now is either lash out in anger or plug your fingers in your ears, clamp down on your heart, and try to ignore the problem into nonexistence. Like it or not, this now must be dealt with for your health, your husband's health, and the health of your marriage.

Remember, as well, that you do not have to suffer through this alone. You're already taking positive steps by reading this book—and we want to assure you that you are not the only woman suffering through this type of indignity. We hope you will talk through your feelings with a trusted female friend or family member, and even seek out a qualified marriage counselor to help *you* navigate this time until you regain trust and restore your marriage.

So back to the specific question that I (Craig) hear all the time, "Should I confront him or catch him?" My answer is *neither.* Confrontation or catching him might feel good by giving you the moral high ground, but the question you need to be asking yourself is, *Do I want to be personally right or relationally whole?*

Assuming you want to be relationally whole, what do you do?

You broach the subject as calmly as you can. Yes, you're hurt. Yes, you're angry. After all, this is a type of betrayal. But I'm going to go out on a limb and say that your husband probably *hates this* about himself and *loves you* deeply.

So I know this is hard, but instead of looking at porn usage as solely a betrayal, see it as a sickness. Your husband is in ill health, sexually. If he was physically ill and was in despair over it, would you be angry and confront him, or would you have empathy for him? I'm guessing it's the latter. The same reasoning applies here: if he's using porn and hates the fact that he does, it will likely help you to at least try to look at your husband not as a betrayer nor as a victim, but as a person who is sick and needs help.

With that in mind, talk to him. You can say something like, "Honey, I've found out about something. I know you've been looking at porn, and while I'm hurt and angry, I still love you and want to see you in a healthy place sexually. Let's talk about this." Likely his eyes will go wide, his face will go deathly pale, and his mouth will suddenly feel stuffed with cotton, but I bet he will feel a tremendous sense of relief that his secret is out. You may need to give him a bit of time before he will be able to talk about it in a meaningful way.

Depending on how far into porn use he has gone, it is possible that the consequences could be serious. It is possible that rebuilding your marriage and the trust essential to it will take a lot of work. Porn use is an insidious disease that can take a long recovery time. But with good help, good information, a lot of good conversations, and good boundaries, your marriage can and will be restored to an even greater place than it's ever been. If you'd like to learn more about the kinds of healing resources that are available and how you can obtain them, please check out MenAreVisual.com/resources or directly at XXXchurch.com.

My son is the one who has the porn problem, not my husband. What do I do?

I believe that you should do the same things we have suggested you do for your husband, but with one exception. With your husband's porn use, I suggested that he, your husband, come up with a plan for moving forward that you and he can discuss and be in agreement over. With your son, it has to be different.

Remember that he lives under your roof and is expected to

abide by your rules. You can pull the plug on (or set time limits on) the Internet, you can cut the cable television, you can trade his smartphone for a dumb phone or eliminate the data plan so he can't go on the Internet. Sure, he can go around you and to a friend's house, but the more you control what goes on in your house, the better. Don't be afraid to stand firm and set consequences and restrictions for your son.

But just as with a husband, it is absolutely vital that you have compassion at the same time. You want, if at all possible, to reach your son's *heart*.

Also, with younger people, the clock ticks more quickly when it comes to addressing the issue: if he's not yet slid into a huge problem, what you do now (or don't do) can affect the rest of his life. So do not delay! The most important thing is to get your son help from someone who is used to walking men and boys through the process of getting free from this type of destructive pattern.

My son has searched the words *big boobs* on the Internet. What do I do?

Be reassured that your son's interest in voluptuous female anatomy is nothing new. In fact, I firmly believe God designed young men to take an interest in the visual aspects of the opposite sex in order to inspire them to find a loving, stable, committed, supportive marriage relationship. It is through relationship that your son will become the man he is supposed to be, and to "be fruitful and multiply."

Anthropologists tell us that part of the way a boy does that is by subconsciously assessing the various characteristics of a woman that would be valuable in caring for his offspring. Like breasts.

Of course, he doesn't generally realize this is what's going on. All he knows is that looking at breasts makes him feel good down south.

Men have been extolling the virtues of breasts as long as there have been men and breasts. We even see this in the Bible! Look no further than the book of Song of Solomon, where Solomon, the wisest man who has ever lived, sings the praises of his lover's breasts many times.[27]

So your son's desire to see the gifts that God has bestowed on women is actually a perfectly natural and healthy desire. There is nothing wrong with this desire itself, and we must not make our son feel that there is!

However.

The problem arises when your son decides to investigate this God-given desire before he's emotionally ready for it, and when he decides to investigate it outside of the marriage covenant. He is a turbulent sea of hormones that are provoking his curiosity and trying to get him to have a good thing—the sexual experience of marriage—in a bad way.

It is crucial to understand that your son is thinking about these things, whether you want him to or not, and whether he is Googling them or not. *This doesn't make him a pervert. It makes him a human male.* (One of the counselors who reviewed this book for us highlighted the last two sentences and said, "Can you make this bold, underlined, italics, and two font sizes larger?!") Your son has been gifted by God with a desire for his eventual wife. He simply must learn how to channel this desire into outlets that will help him get a handle on it and control it so that it doesn't control him. And searching "boobs" on the Internet is a signal that he is feeding that desire at the wrong time, instead of controlling it.

The best thing you can do now is talk to your son about his activity and about how God has wired him to find these things intriguing. Then discuss the dangers that are on the Internet, making sure to keep the discussion age appropriate. If you haven't already talked to your son about sex-related issues, now's the time, because he's obviously interested. Your husband will also need to talk with him about pornography, about its dangers, and about tactics to avoid it online and in the real world.

And you need to install filtering or accountability software on all your Internet-linked devices. I (Craig) recommend downloading our X3watch software. I have gone as far as installing a device called Circle that creates a safe, filtered Internet connection for all the devices at our house, as well as the devices of all my kids' friends who come over who don't have filtering software on their phones. (We have so many resources at MenAreVisual.com/resources that will help you, along with a discount code for that Circle device. There is even a talk I did called "How to Talk to Your Kids About Sex and Porn" that you can watch.)

It would also be good to start talking to your son about your expectations for the ways he needs to view women. Because men are wired to seek out women visually, it's very easy for them to look at women as objects that have been placed in front of them specifically for their viewing pleasure. You want to knock that nonsense down quickly and reinforce to your son that women are, in fact, *people,* just like he is. He needs to respect the girls and women around him. Communicate that there is far more to women than their appearance and he needs to see them for more than just their looks. When you hear teenage boys laughing and joking in a way that you think makes a girl an object, challenge that. ("Would you want your buddies to talk about your sister that way?") Make him *think.*

But what if I don't have a man I respect available for the most important and awkward talks?

If your husband is not available for such a talk—for example, if you're a single mom—we still recommend that you have a trustworthy adult male have the initial talk with your son. Honestly, there are just some things boys don't want to hear from their moms, and learning about sex or porn is one of them. Find an uncle, a pastor, or a youth leader from church who can sit down with your son and guide him as he takes his first steps down this important rite of passage.

After that point, you can't run from this. Dig into this instead of avoiding it and being scared. You can show your son by your calm, matter-of-fact manner that it doesn't have to be awkward to talk about.

But what if my husband won't talk to our son?

Find out why he won't. If he has a real reason, you may not agree with that reason but you have to acknowledge that since you're not a man, he may have a better perspective on this. For example, maybe your husband thinks that your son is still too innocent and that computer restrictions are sufficient right now. Maybe he has another reason why he feels it is important to wait. But if your husband is just embarrassed or doesn't know what to do, then give him an out and ask, "Is there another way we can do this? Can we find a book you can use to go over this with him? Do you want me to do it?"

The one thing you can't do, unless you're sure there's a real problem with either your husband (which makes him the wrong person to have the talk) or your son (which makes talking soon essential), is to say, "Either you do it or I will." At least if you want to preserve your marriage. Be careful that you're not simply distrusting your husband and trying to run the show.

But if your husband is truly an avoider, if there is concrete evidence of a real problem, and if your son evidences a real pattern of searching out dangerous images—all of which could cause a lifetime of problems—then someone needs to take action soon. But make sure you have a good plan first. Otherwise, you probably won't help your son, and all you're going to do is stir things up both for him and your husband.

See if there's another man your husband respects who can talk to your husband about this. Or if he still won't be convinced, perhaps you can work with another man who is an authority in your son's life anyway—like a youth pastor—to talk to your son. And if you are the one who is going to talk to your son, get advice from other men. Learn what needs to be said and how to say it. You've got to be able to be sure you can provide what your son actually needs.

You may also want to seek out a skilled marriage counselor, because this has now become a marriage issue as well.

What if it has become a real problem for my son?

If your son has a lengthy history of wayward Google searches, long showers with waterproof video devices, or other issues, then you need to take some extra precautions. Not just by putting the computer in the living room (that's a given), but by making him keep all his gaming or mobile devices in some community area of your home, by allowing you to take those devices into your own bedroom overnight, and by routinely reviewing his text messages and activity.

As we've mentioned before, XXXchurch has also developed software called X3watch that monitors online activity. When that computer or device is used to visit a questionable site, a report gets e-mailed to an accountability partner who then knows what's happened. It's an effective deterrent for a son that will help him develop self-control while online.

And let's not ignore that there are far more dangerous traps than just pornography. In today's world a large percentage of the apps that your kids have on their phones or iPods allow interaction with other real human beings. A ton of apps are built for the sole purpose of doing things in private with, or communicating and hooking up with, real people. I am not trying to scare you, but it is not uncommon for thirteen-year-old girls on widely used picture-sharing apps to be asked for pictures of their breasts—and many are fine complying. Understand what your kids are doing online and who they are interacting with. Get more information on this at iParent.tv.

My seven-year-old son accidentally saw pornographic images online. What do I do? Is there any way I can minimize the damage of those images?

This one is tough. The good thing is that your seven-year-old is innocent enough that these images probably won't have staying power, but there's no guarantee. He still doesn't really know what sex is, so you have the opportunity to take the lead here to minimize potential harm.

First off, once again, *try not to freak out about it.* I (Craig) know this sounds counterintuitive, but if you make a big deal out of it, then it can become a big deal. Children follow our lead in knowing what's important and what isn't, so they're always looking at us and mimicking our behavior and responses to things. If you turn this into a big production, your son may think, *Oh, this is important. I should probably remember this.*

That said, you also don't want to undersell it. After all, you want him to think twice about trying to find more of those kinds of images! You know your child better than anyone else, so play it cool. Then if you start to notice some behavioral changes or if he starts asking questions he's never asked before, you can calmly and gently explain—at his level of understanding—that he saw something meant for grownups and not kids. This is a chance to talk about privacy, modesty, and God's design to keep our bodies for marriage.

And if it's any comfort to you, you can always remember my story of seeing pornography when I was young, knowing pretty much what it was, and still retaining a healthy sexuality from that time forward. One exposure to porn will not turn your son into a raging, lust-filled monster who consumes everything with an insatiable appetite. Just keep it honest, stay aware, keep it cool, and keep it together, and he should be fine.

My husband wants to go to strip clubs, even though I hate the idea. Am I just uptight, and is it okay for him to do this?

There is not a universe, known or unknown, where visiting a strip club is okay. Strip clubs are dehumanizing, both for the patrons and for the dancers, and I (Craig) know because one aspect of our work through XXXchurch's sister ministry, StripChurch.com, is doing ministry in these strip club environments almost every day, around the world.

So now we have to wonder, why would your husband be asking you this question? If he is trying to convince you that strip clubs are harmless, then there is definitely a deeper issue below the surface of that request, and the two of you need to work together—probably with the help of a qualified marriage counselor.

Perhaps your husband is trying to get you to go along with the idea of his going out to a strip club, but he shouldn't be pushing you that way in the first place. That isn't the way marriage works. Instead, he should be honoring your feelings about the sacredness of your sexual relationship. This isn't like a disagreement over pizza toppings—this is a deeply intimate, intensely private aspect of your relationship that you share only with one another. That your husband would be contemplating something as overtly out of line as a strip club indicates that he needs outside assistance to gain a healthier perspective on his own sexuality and on the sexual relationship he shares with you.

Or maybe he hasn't talked to you about strip clubs but you find he's been visiting them. In that case, treat it just as if you've caught him viewing porn, and address it as we suggest above.

In any of these cases, there are much bigger issues at play here than your husband's visual nature. You should address those issues together with a trusted friend, pastor, or marriage counselor.

Suddenly, my husband wants to try new things in the bedroom that make me uncomfortable. What do I do?

If your husband is attempting to try things with you during sex that you are uncomfortable with, you are completely within your bounds to tell him exactly that and have an honest talk with him about it. It may be that he is completely unaware of how it makes you feel. If that's the case, he'll likely set it aside in order to respect you and the covenant you renew every time you're intimate with one another.

If he won't listen or still tries to pressure you into things that you don't want to do, then it is very possible that your husband has a deeper issue he needs to deal with. Ask yourself these two questions.

First, why must he insist on doing this, when he knows how you feel about it? If he is unwilling to respect your feelings on this issue, then it's time to have a deeper talk. If you find you cannot resolve the issue, you might need to head to counseling.

But second, and more specifically, why is he asking for this particular new fantasy to play out, and where did that fantasy come from? Odd positions or practices that make you feel uncomfortable can be a major red flag as far as porn is concerned. Yes, men have sexually creative minds, but they don't always invent these things on the spur of the moment—sometimes men see things in porn that they want to try with their wives. You may need to investigate and find out where he's getting all these ideas from. You should know that some types of pornography today can drive men to extremes. Some of the stuff that men are watching online is not like the *Playboy* magazines of old; it can be very graphic and hardcore in nature. If he is suggesting unusual things in the bedroom, I (Craig) feel there is a strong possibility that he is looking at pornography. So go back to the principles we laid out throughout this book and have a conversation with him about his visual nature.

My husband wants to record a video of us having sex. Should I?

Just the fact that you're asking the question shows your discomfort with the idea—and rightly so. Maybe you're worried about where the video will go or whether anyone other than your husband will see it. And to be honest, in an age where *nothing* digital is safe from hacking, that is a legitimate concern. But in addition, now your discomfort has come between you and your husband. And the larger question isn't about the video; it's about whether this behavior is beneficial.

So again, I (Craig) would ask, why would your husband want to do this? What is he hoping to use it for? Where will this video go, and what would he (and you) do if someone else were to see it? I (Shaunti) know of a case where a married couple's *deleted* sex video was, it turns out, still backed up in the cloud somewhere, found by a hacker, and posted far and wide on porn sites.

All these concerns about recorded sex create worry, and the

minute you start to worry, that's when something has come between you and your husband. Something has intruded on the sexual covenant you have with one another, and this time it's far too easy to share with the rest of the world.

Remember, sex is not entirely about the physical act. Yes, there is pleasure to be had, and that is indeed one very enjoyable facet of sexuality, but it is not all there is to it. When you and your husband have sex, you are creating an atmosphere of intimacy, something that builds your relationship little by little; the act of sex does not, in itself, capture the entirety of your sex life.

But your husband, as a visual person, is likely not going to watch that video and call to mind the emotional bond the two of you had in that moment, the intimacy and closeness you created. No, the chances are he's going to be watching something else you created together: *a homemade porn movie.*

In my (Craig's) opinion, this is just too dangerous a line to be walking. We once had someone ask this because her husband was deploying on military duty and wanted to have a little something of her to take with him overseas, and while we understand the thought behind it and applaud this husband for his ingenuity in trying to maintain his sexual relationship with his wife while deployed, we simply cannot endorse bringing a video camera into the bedroom. I know a lot of women are going to struggle with the uncomfortable nature of having sex with the lights on, let alone a video camera in the room.

And it goes without saying that if your husband tries to convince you that making a video with him will help keep him from looking at porn, well, he needs to come up with other ways to keep from looking at porn and stop pressuring you to do something you don't want to do.

We have bigger problems than just occasional porn use. (For example: My husband is a sex addict. Or, my husband cheated on me.) What now?

Sadly, we know that some of you will be in this category. But as we said at the outset, the most serious ends of the spectrum go beyond what we can tackle here. We urge you to immediately seek out specialized help from qualified counselors and ministries that target your particular concern. The resources at MenAreVisual.com will at least give you a starting point for specialized places to look and get referrals.

Restoration doesn't usually just spontaneously happen. It's going to take a lot of hard work, and so you're going to need the aid of someone who has walked this road with dozens or hundreds of couples like you. Please don't try to shoulder this burden on your own.

In addition to a marriage counselor, it's also a good idea to invite at least one other couple into your restoration process, someone who can help keep both of you accountable to one another, who can listen to you when you need to think things through out loud, who can provide a solid shoulder to cry on, and who can encourage you in the dry times when motivation is thin.

Most of all, have hope. We have both seen many couples come back from the worst imaginable situations, and you can too. Your marriage is worth fighting for.

I thought it was my son on porn sites, but it was actually my daughter. What do I do?

So, we just spent the whole book talking about men and how men are visual and different from women, then we drop this "What about my visual daughter?" bomb near the end of the book. What are we thinking?

To be honest, I (Craig) put this question in here because I want to let you know about a shift I see in the next generation. At an alarming rate, girls are buying into the lie that porn is okay, even cool. They are seeing what happens when they wear the skimpy outfits. They see the looks they get, or the likes their Instagram accounts get when they post a provocative photo. They even understand and accept much of what we shared in this book—except the idea that porn is something to be cautious about. They have an easier time with the information than you do because they have been exposed to it since they were very young . . . and, all too often, are interested in it themselves.

One in three visitors to porn sites are now women. Do I believe girls are visually stimulated as much as guys? Most of them, no, but that doesn't mean they are not interested or not watching. And research is suggesting that they are rewiring their brains in the process. A lot of them want to be the girl who supports her boyfriend's habit rather than the one who is questioning him or pushing him to be honorable. I just don't want you to put this book down and forget about your girls. Girls are facing a number of challenges these days, and their curiosity might eventually lead them to these sites.

And given those facts, it is just as important that you are aware of a daughter's interests and just as determined to be proactive about walking your daughter through this minefield well. As one example, here is an e-mail I recently received:

Craig,

This evening we found porn on our nine-year-old daughter's iPad. After first lying to us, she said that a girl in school told her about the site and she did not know what it was, so that is why she looked it up. But apparently she has

viewed this site a lot since her classmate told her about it
three weeks ago.

Our daughter still believes in Santa Claus; she is
extremely young minded and very naive. As parents, what
should we do from here?

As you can imagine, I was more than a little troubled by this
e-mail, but I was hopeful too. These parents were on top of the issue
and were engaging their daughter in conversation about it. And that
matters more than anything else. I made contact with this family
and shared my thoughts with them.

First off, don't worry. I know you feel like your daughter has
seen everything there is to see and has been robbed of every
ounce of her innocence, but I assure you this isn't the case.
Your daughter doesn't know everything now—in fact, it's
quite the opposite; she doesn't know *anything*. Not anything
that's real.

But since this is going on, there's a major urgency for you
to talk with her about what she's seen and what it's doing
within her heart and mind. Don't run away from this opportunity, but lovingly and calmly discuss this issue with her. Don't
shame her and don't punish her, because she likely didn't know
she was doing something wrong. This does not have to be the
end of the world for her innocence, as much as it may seem
like it. Yes, it's a bad situation, but you can get through it.

The bright side of this particular situation is that,
because it happened to your daughter at a young age, you're
still in a place to handle it before it can become a bigger issue.
She's still impressionable, she still looks up to you, and she

still wants your guidance and input. If this had happened when your daughter was a teenager, she would probably still look up to you, but she would be more independent in terms of what she decided to do about it.

So believe it or not, this can be a positive experience. Now you have the wisdom and experience to be involved with your daughter in all the important conversations about her sexuality and all that entails—and you get to start teaching her those lessons at an age when she'll be more receptive to what you have to say. But again, it's all about creating and sustaining the dialogue.

I suggest that any parent in this situation also seek out a qualified children's counselor for some specific help in walking through it over the coming weeks.

How likely is it that my marriage can recover after a porn problem?

It's very likely. Look, I (Craig) have seen so many marriages hit the rocks as a result of porn, and I've seen—over and over again—those marriages restored. And not back to the prior level, either; in our experience with XXXchurch, the majority of the couples we've worked with have expressed that their marriages are better than they were before.

And that makes sense. Because when porn is involved in a marriage, it gets in the way of true, long-lasting intimacy. It's a secret. It's a barrier. It prevents husbands and wives from knowing one another fully. So while acknowledging a porn problem can be heartrending and dealing with it can be some of the hardest work you've ever done as a couple, *it is worth it.*

Because then the barrier is gone, and there's one less thing standing between the two of you and complete oneness. The happiness and joy that do eventually come around in the midst of the struggle are so much richer and deeper than what you can imagine. I don't know about you, but to me, that sounds like something worth fighting for.

Should I let my daughter wear a bikini?

That has to be up to you. There are some logistical, fairness, and family issues to consider, and let's tackle those first. With bikini swimsuits being the overwhelming norm for girls today (at least in the US and other western countries), any decision for your daughter to cover up a bit more by wearing a tankini or a one-piece swimsuit will take a purposeful effort to find the right swim gear and a determination to stick with it despite pushback—either protests from your child who will (at least in most cases) be very much in the minority, from peer pressure, or from your own weariness at fighting the "But why not, Mom?!" battle. Or even from the fact that it simply can be just plain difficult to find clothes today that cover enough real estate, much less bathing suits! (My [Craig's] daughter is ten, and I joke that I am buying her future teenage outfits now because each year girls seem to wear less and less clothing, so I can't imagine how skimpy bathing suits and shorts and dresses will be by the time she is a teenager.)

It is important to say that both of us are acquainted with many caring fathers who know all too well the thoughts that will be in the minds of the nearby men and boys, and yet they do not feel it is right to prohibit their teenage daughters from wearing a bikini. In many cases, these fathers do not feel it is fair to their daughter to have to be different and not feel like she fits in simply because the guys around her will be tempted to fantasize about her later in their room at night.

As one father of a beautiful fifteen-year-old told me (Shaunti), "Look, that can and will happen with one-piece swimsuits too. After all, there were millions of men that would masturbate to mental images of Pamela Anderson from *Baywatch,* and she was wearing a one-piece. I just don't think it's fair to my daughter to deny her ability to fit in—or even to make her uncomfortable for sticking out in her one-piece—just because of how guys will think about her, when many of them would think about her in that way anyway."

Other families, of course, make the opposite decision.

But we would argue that all those issues, while important to consider, should not be the *primary* variables considered when making this decision. Like all awkward challenges in a culture that was never supposed to be this way, the main question to ask yourself (and for your daughter to ask herself) is, what decision would most delight the heart of God? More specifically, if your daughter is trying to love the Lord her God and love her neighbor as herself, which choice will reflect that best?

In my (Shaunti's) family, my husband and I pray about this each year. At the moment, our fifteen-year-old daughter continues to hope that we will change our minds and let her wear a bikini. But up to this point, we continue to feel that her wearing a one-piece suit or a tankini in public will show that she understands and wants to honor the boys around her, just as she wants them to honor her. For now, due to her age, this is a requirement. But we are praying that as she quickly matures into a young woman who makes her own choices, she will continue on that path.

If that is an error on our part, we feel that at least it is erring on the side of caution. For any girl, the risk of a desire to fit in and wear the cute bikini is the risk that she will err on the side of her wanting to do what she wants to do, regardless of the impact on the guys around her. So for us, at least for now, we feel this caution is the path that is more likely to teach her to honor God.

You may feel differently. We know many families that deeply want to honor God in all things and yet have come to a different conclusion. So you will have to pray about it, think it through with the full knowledge of how the male mind works, and make the choice that you feel is right for your family, your daughter, and your situation.

Someone just showed me that my teenage daughter posed in a sexy, skimpy outfit for her social media profile picture, and I'm extremely uncomfortable with that. What do I do?

Obviously, if she's legally an adult, out of your house (a college student, for example), and paying her own bills, you can't make her do anything differently. But if she is still living under your roof, even if she is a senior in high school and about to leave the nest, you are still the authority in her life. That means you must be completely aware of her social media use, presumably so you see everything that her friends see. Many parents set up alerts so they are notified every time their kids post a status update, a new picture, or anything else. Doing that will not only allow you to stay much more involved in the day-to-day aspects of your child's life, it will also ensure you see a picture like this when it first goes up. Then you can talk to her about it right away and require that she make a different decision.

But she will need to understand *why* you are requiring that. It sounds like your daughter may need to come to grips with understanding what goes through the mind of the guys who see her picture, what it says to the world that she would use that picture, and why she is doing it in the first place.

The trend on social media these days is overly revealing selfies.

Females—from teenagers to grown women—might post photos of themselves in tight workout clothes that show off their chests, focusing all attention on their bodies. I (Craig) found out one of my son's Instagram friends had over two thousand followers. I figured she was a thriving, new, young movie star. No. Just a fifteen-year-old girl who shows a lot of skin and in turn has a lot of followers. Parents, please wake up! This behavior is starting at early ages: girls are seeking attention, approval, and acceptance in inappropriate ways. Talk to your girls. Help them to see the dangers of what they're doing. Help them to respect not only themselves but also their social media friends. Help them to honor God with their lives. Just as we all should.

• • • • •

In the end, as you have seen with so many of the issues discussed in this book, we can share knowledge, be supportive, learn how to listen, set boundaries, and try lots of other things, but ultimately the action that matters most is to trust and rely on the God who created us and our men in the first place. He is the only one who can actually change a heart. Including ours.

Thanks for Taking the Journey

Ladies, we've reached the end of this particular journey into the minds of men. Thanks for going on this adventure with us. We hope this isn't the end of your own journey to greater understanding, wisdom, and hope.

No matter what is going on in your relationship with the males in your life, we hope you have a vision for the fact that the way God created them is good.

We hope you have a sense for just how much the man or boy in your life wants to be able to look to you for calm, unwavering support and understanding.

And we hope you have a vision for just how beautiful a relationship can be once people come through a challenging time with much greater understanding, intimacy, and trust.

Ultimately, as you continue to try to see life through the eyes of your man, as the Bible puts it,

I pray that the eyes of your heart may be enlightened, so that you will know what is the hope of His calling, what are the riches of the glory of His inheritance in the saints, and what is the surpassing greatness of His power toward us who believe.[28]

● ● ● ● ●

Oh, one last thing. You know the many times we annoyingly asked you to wait to talk to your husband or son until you'd reached the end of the book? Well . . .

You've reached the **end** of the book!

Blessings on your discussions!

Acknowledgments

This book isn't just written by the two of us but by the combined efforts of many hundreds of stakeholders across both of our ministries, on opposite sides of the country, and two very widely scattered networks of colleagues, associates, mentors, counselors, readers, listeners, friends, and family.

Since there is no way to properly thank everyone, let us just say that we are immensely grateful to those without whom this book would not exist:

- The extraordinary staff and team members of our two ministries, who go far beyond just doing a great job and truly work "as unto the Lord" each day with a deep desire to see people thrive in their lives and marriages.

- The key advisors in our lives, including literary agent Esther Fedorkevich, who originally came up with the idea for the book.

- The dozens of dedicated people who helped conduct the research with such professional skill and rigor over many years.

- The thousands of men and women who provided research input.

- The dozens of professional counselors, therapists, specialists, pastors, lay leaders, wives, husbands, moms, and dads who reviewed the book, to help us try to create something that would be not only accurate but also useful. We especially want to thank Michael

Sytsma of Building Intimate Marriages (Intimate Marriage.org), Michael Todd Wilson of Intentional Hearts (IntentionalHearts.com), and Steven Luff of FaithAndSexCenter.com for the many hours they spent providing detailed feedback and counsel.

- The many friends and extended family who encouraged, counseled, challenged, and held us up during the years that this book was in the creation process. Special thanks to our prayer teams who did the real work, especially to J. R. Roberson for the title of the book.

- The wonderful folks at Waterbrook Multnomah and the larger Penguin Random House family, especially our tremendous editors, Dave Kopp and Susan Tjaden. A note from Shaunti: Dave, my friend, your remarkable insight has been a huge part of nearly every book I've written in the last eleven years. God has used you in mighty ways in my life, Jeff's life, and the lives of millions more. We know He will continue to. But we sure miss you, brother.

- The beautiful people in our immediate and extended families. From Shaunti: To my amazing family, especially my husband Jeff and our two sweet kids, you are the best part of my life and I am so grateful for you. From Craig: Jeanette, Nolan, and Elise, you guys are the greatest part of my days and everything to me.

- Most important, we are grateful to the One to whom we owe it all, the One who is waiting for that day when *all* will be made right. Thank You for letting us be a small part of Your Great Story.

Notes

1. It is important to note that there is a wide range of normal for men, just as for women, but that this book will not be able to address all those cases. For example, according to multiple sex therapists I (Shaunti) have spoken with, in roughly 20 percent of relationships, the woman has more sexual desire than the man—and those men are still on the spectrum of what is normal.

2. Madhura Ingalhalikar, Alex Smith, Drew Parker, Theodore D. Satterthwaite, Mark A. Elliott, Kosha Ruparel, Hakon Hakonarson, Raquel E. Gur, Ruben C. Gur, and Ragini Verma, "Sex Differences in the Structural Connectome of the Human Brain," *Proceedings of the National Academy of Sciences* (PNAS) 111, no. 2 (January 14, 2014): 823, www.pnas.org /content/111/2/823.

3. Larry Cahill, "Fundamental Sex Difference in Human Brain Architecture," *Proceedings of the National Academy of Sciences* (PNAS) 111, no. 2 (January 14, 2014): 577, www.pnas.org /content/111/2/577.full.

4. The "to one degree or another" qualification is key. Some men will fit the brain wiring described in this chapter in nearly all respects; others will fit some parts of it, but not all. Again, although there is very definitely a male type of brain wiring, there are wide differences among individual men.

5. Tim Koscik, Dan O'Leary, David J. Moser, Nancy C. Andreasen, and Peg Nopoulos, "Sex Differences in Parietal Lobe

Morphology: Relationship to Mental Rotation Performance,"
Brain and Cognition 69, no. 3: 451–59.

6. Michael Gurian, *What Could He Be Thinking?* (New York:
St. Martin's Press, 2003), 107–109.

7. A group of scientists from Massachusetts General Hospital,
Harvard Medical School, and Massachusetts Institute of
Technology found through functional MRI scans (fMRIs)
that men's brains are affected at a very primal level when they
look at pictures of women they perceive as attractive. (Itzhak
Aharon, Nancy Etcoff, Dan Ariely, Chris F. Chabris, Ethan
O'Connor, and Hans C. Breiter, "Beautiful Faces Have
Variable Reward Value: fMRI and Behavioral Evidence,"
Neuron 32, no. 3 [November 8, 2001]: 537–51.) As ABC's
John Stossel put it when he reported on this study in 2002,
"The same part of the brain [the nucleus accumbens] lights
up when a young man sees a picture of a beautiful woman as
when a hungry person sees food, or a gambler eyes cash, or a
drug addict sees a fix." (John Stossel, "The Ugly Truth About
Beauty," August 23, 2002, http://abcnews.go.com/2020
/story?id=123853.)

8. As David M. Buss, a professor of psychology at the University
of Texas at Austin, says, "Telling men not to become aroused
by signs of beauty, youth, and health is like telling them not to
experience sugar as sweet." David M. Buss, *The Evolution of
Desire* (New York: Basic Books, 1994), 71.

9. No one knows the exact percentage of women who are more
visually wired than is typical for the female gender, but as
Michael Gurian explains in his book *What Could He Be
Thinking?*, researchers believe up to 25 percent of the popula-
tion has "bridge brains"—brains that include characteristics

common to the opposite sex. In this case, higher levels of testosterone are a likely factor in a higher visual orientation. Also, just as there is a wide range of normal among men, there is a wide range among women as well. If you find yourself identifying with many of the descriptions of a man's visual nature, you are probably among those women who have a higher-than-average level of testosterone—and you are just as normal.

10. According to a study by Emory University researchers published in the professional journal *Nature Neuroscience,* when men and women see sexual stimuli, a man's amygdala (which regulates emotion and aggression) and hypothalamus (which primes a hormonal response) are more strongly activated. Stephan Hamann, Rebecca A. Herman, Carla L. Nolan, and Kim Wallen, "Men and Women Differ in Amygdala Response to Visual Sexual Stimuli," *Nature Neuroscience* 7 (2004): 411–16, www.ncbi.nlm.nih.gov/pubmed/15004563.

11. This is an impact of pornography. Researchers from the Max Planck Institute for Human Development in Berlin, Germany, have noted "a link between porn consumption and reductions in brain size and brain activity in response to sexual stimuli." In other words, the more porn people consumed, the smaller the reward centers of their brain and the more limited they were in their capacity to make good decisions. Pornography literally messes with men's heads—to their detriment.

12. Hebrews 4:15, NASB.

13. Some theologians disagree that Jesus suffered any sexual temptation. It's true that the Bible doesn't tell us what His specific temptations were. But the point here is to acknowledge that the existence of the temptation to do something or think

about something is not the same thing as doing it or thinking about it—which is sin.

14. Walt Larimore and Barb Larimore, *His Brain, Her Brain: How Divinely Designed Differences Can Strengthen Your Marriage* (Grand Rapids, MI: Zondervan, 2008), 46–47.

15. Joseph LeDoux, "Emotional Memory Systems in the Brain," *Behavioral Brain Research* 58, nos. 1–2 (December 1993): 69–79; "Emotion, Memory, and the Brain," *Scientific American* (June 1994): 50–57; "Emotion and the Limbic System Concept," *Concepts in Neuroscience* 2 (1991): 169–99.

16. Shaunti Feldhahn, *The Male Factor, Expanded Edition* (Colorado Springs: Multnomah, 2009), 263.

17. When I shared this story with one experienced sex-addiction therapist, he pointed out, "Actually, I don't know of anyone who has been 'delivered' in the way this man thinks, because this is not like alcohol and drugs. Those are substances going into our bodies, and deliverance can happen for some people as God removes the craving for them. But to remove sexual cravings would violate a part of us—our sexuality—that God created. And then you wouldn't be attracted to your wife! A better analogy might be a food addict who will always have that tension. How a food addict deals with food is how someone in this situation deals with sex. That craving is always there. And it should be."

18. Specialized input was provided by many therapists, counselors, and coaches who work in the area of sexual temptation. Dr. Michael Sytsma and Michael Todd Wilson in particular provided extensive information for the book over the course of several years and as we were crafting it, especially during 2014,

via in-depth phone, e-mail, and in-person consultations. Quotes used by permission.

19. Matthew 7:3.

20. Matthew 7:4–5.

21. Philippians 2:4–5, 7–8, NLT.

22. Romans 14:13.

23. Phylicia Masonheimer, "Modesty, Yoga Pants and 5 Myths You Need to Know," August 19, 2013, ChurchLeaders, www .churchleaders.com/pastors/pastor-articles/175460-phylicia -masonheimer-modesty-yoga-pants-and-5-myths-you-need -to-know.html. Used by permission.

24. Romans 7:15, NLT.

25. In this book we are focusing on visual men, but as noted, we recognize that there are visual women who have struggles too. And if you are one of those women, realize you're definitely not alone. There are plenty of resources through XXXchurch that will help you too. And if you have a problem, the suggestions about seeking help and accountability are vital for you as well.

26. "Enjoying Marriage in the Midst of the Grind," FamilyLife Today, Ted Cunningham interview by Bob Lepine and Dennis Rainey, November 10, 2014, http://familylifetoday .com/program/enjoying-marriage-in-the-midst-of-the-grind. "Fun Loving You," FamilyLife Today broadcast interview with Ted Cunningham, copyright © 2014 by FamilyLife. All rights reserved. Used by permission. Edited slightly for clarity.

27. See Song of Solomon 4:5; 7:3; and 7:7 for examples.

28. Ephesians 1:18–19, NASB.

More resources
from Shaunti and Craig

For Women

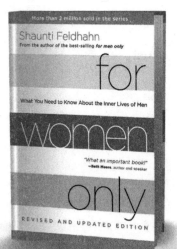

For Men